Colorblind

original images

Joseph Fleming

Colorblind
original images

Decades of being around accomplished talent producing absolutely phenomenal quality work has taught that we are capable of greatness. It is possible to meet our destiny and become it. Experiencing excellence done with such apparent ease and humble selfless gratification is motivation for this collection.

Being colorblind gives an advantage when composing black & white… less confusion.

These selections, from thousands of captures during years of travels, exhibit the lonely freedom of a hidden perspective. All images are presented genuine without edits. Color sacrificed by unique proprietary process.

Original fine art and custom work available.

info@ BEACHNOISE.com

0125

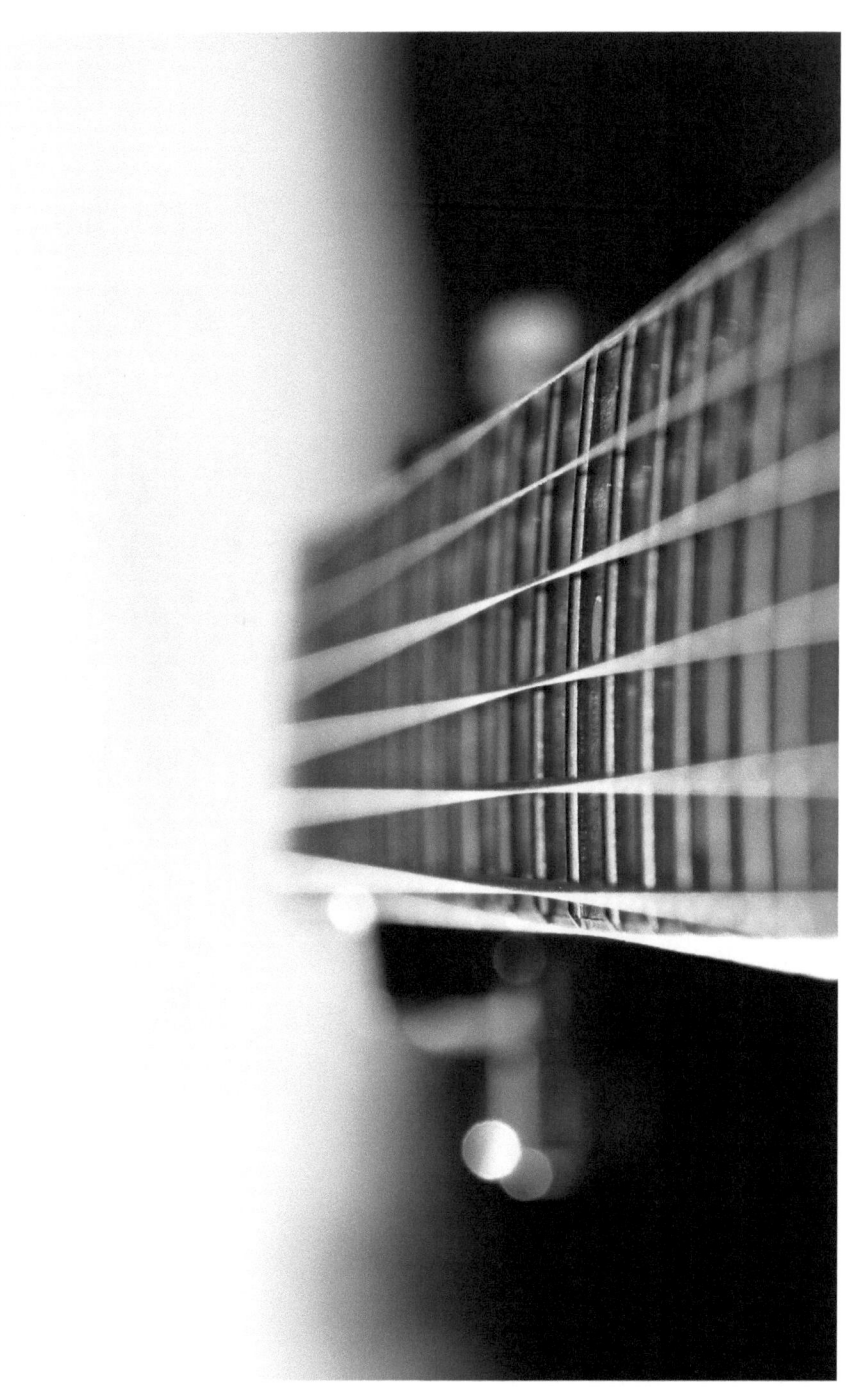

0351

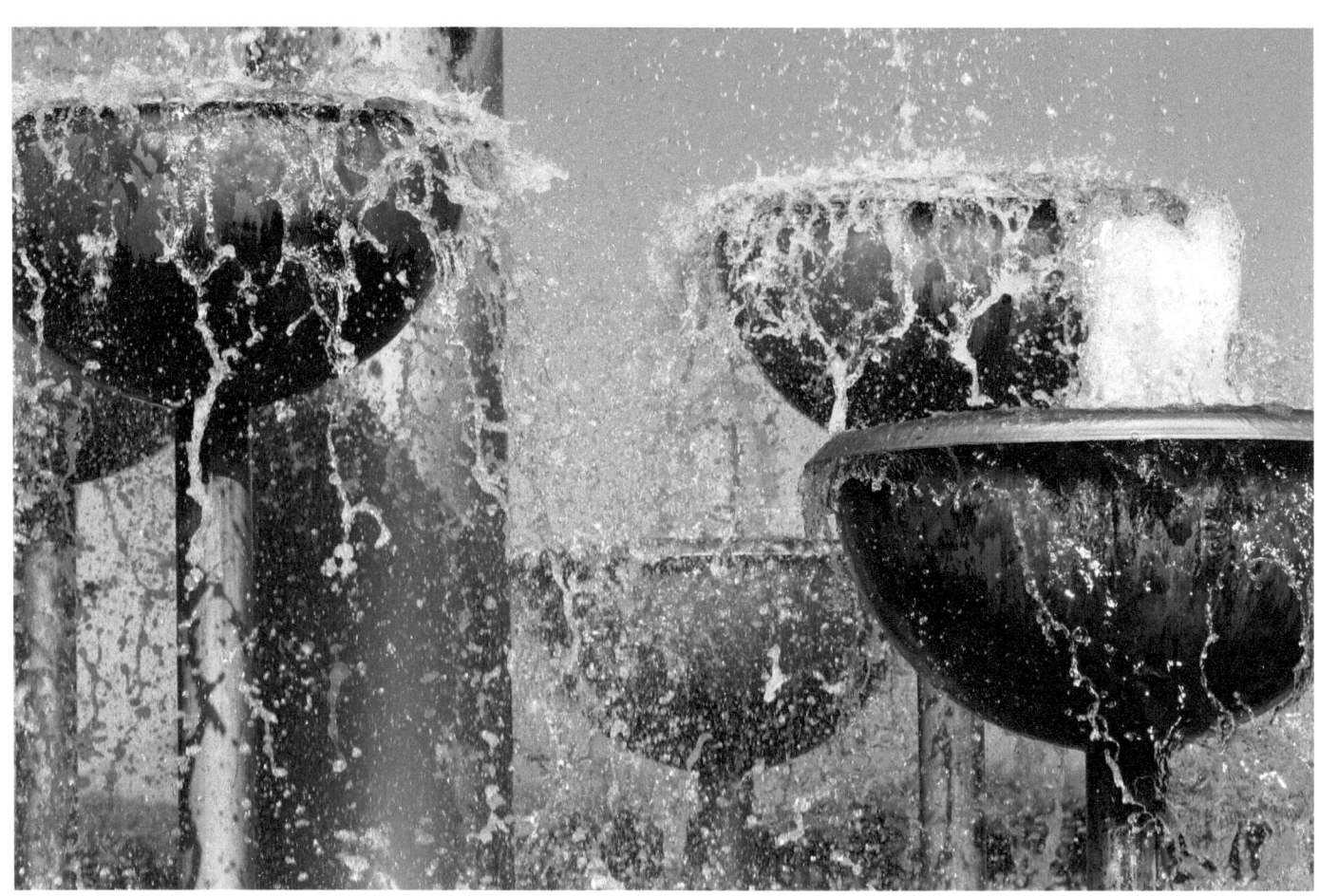

0354

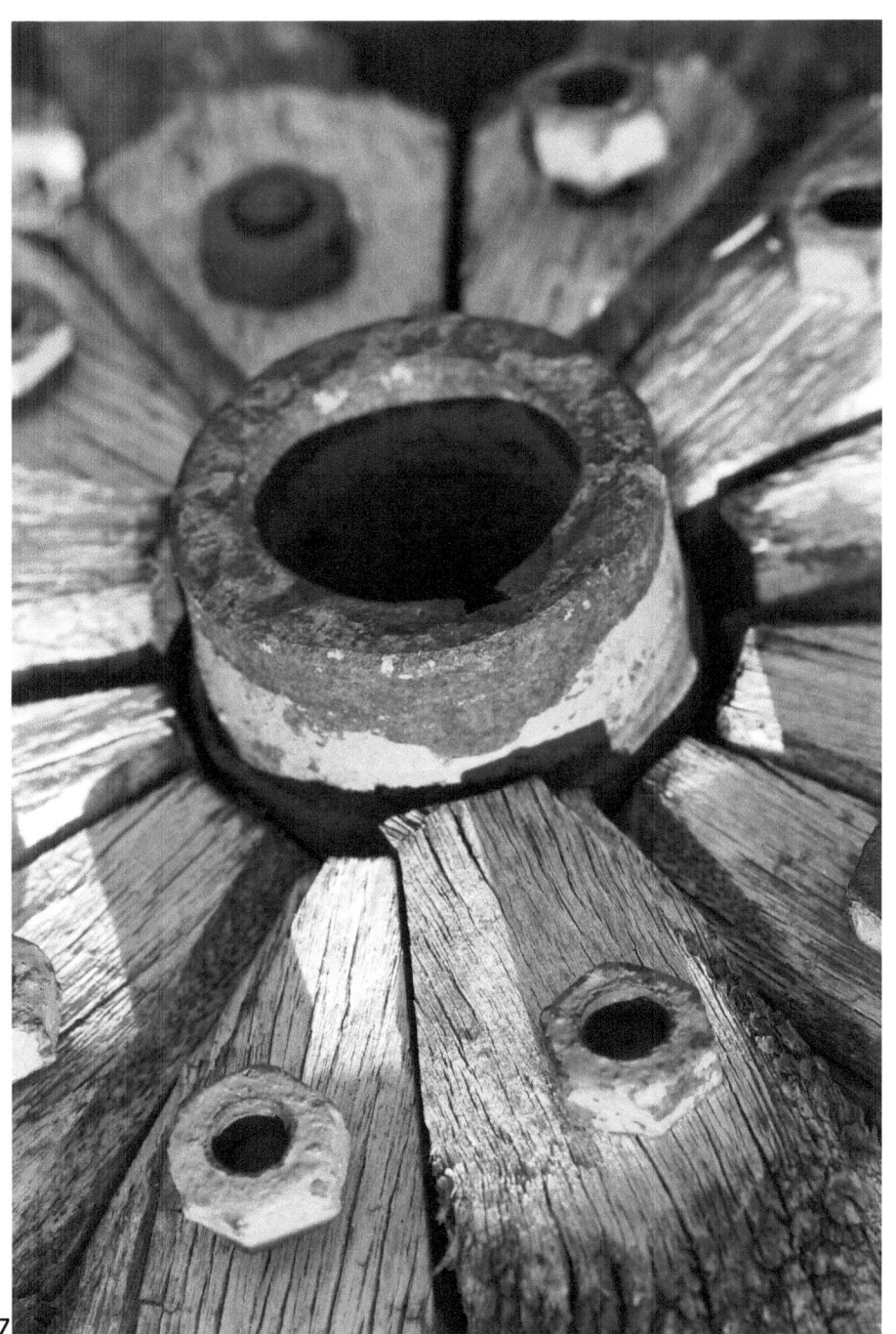

0437

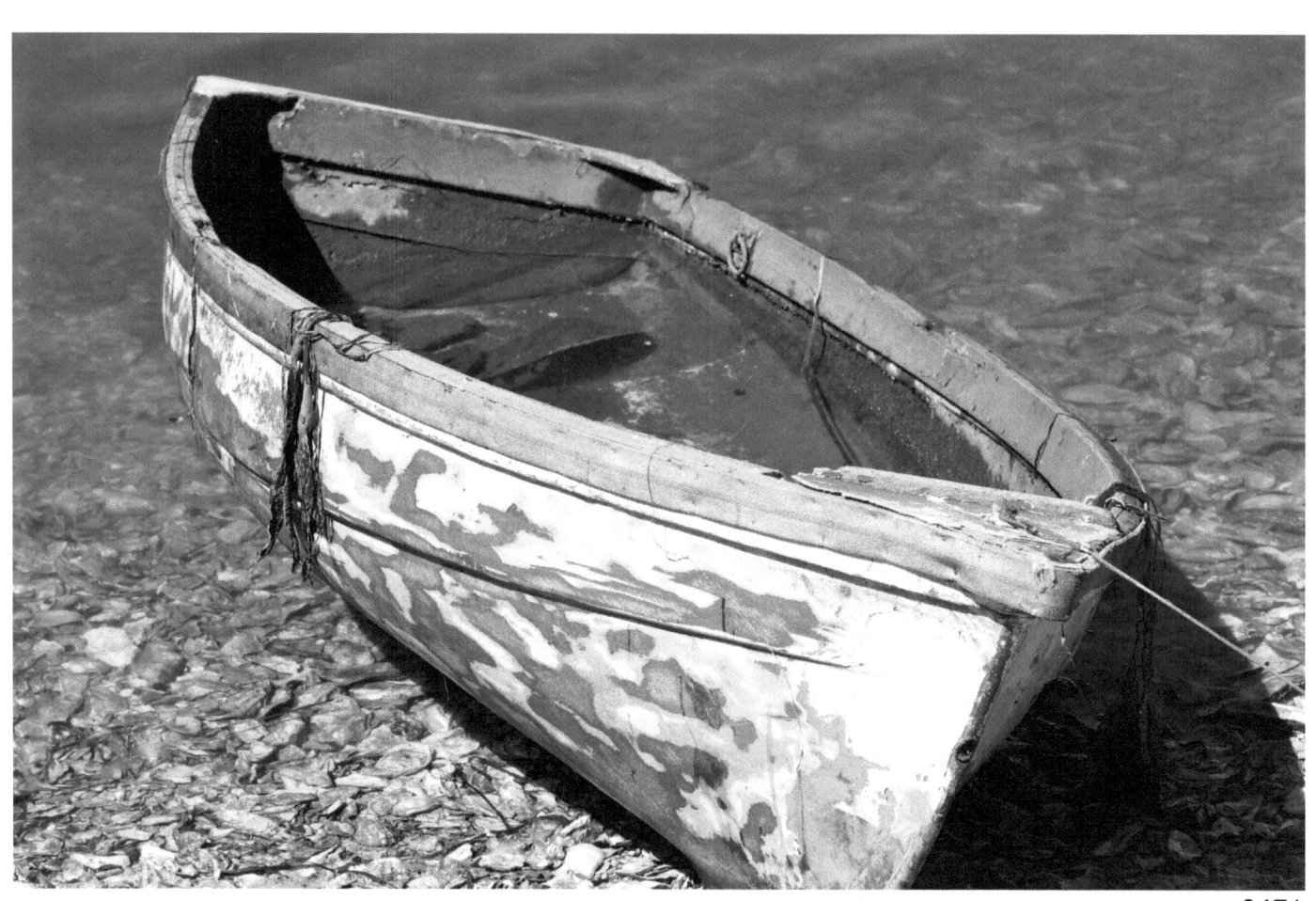

0471

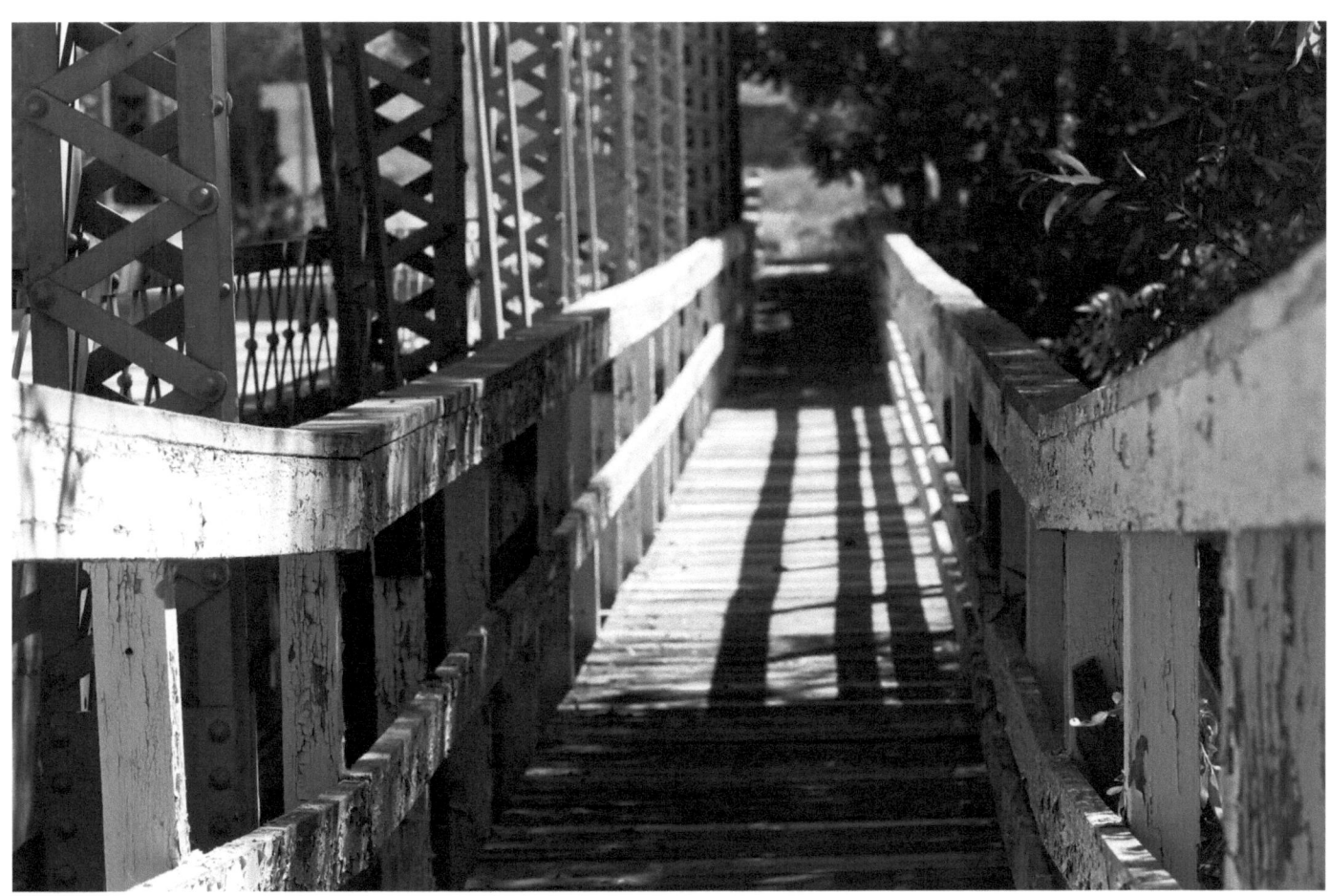

0503

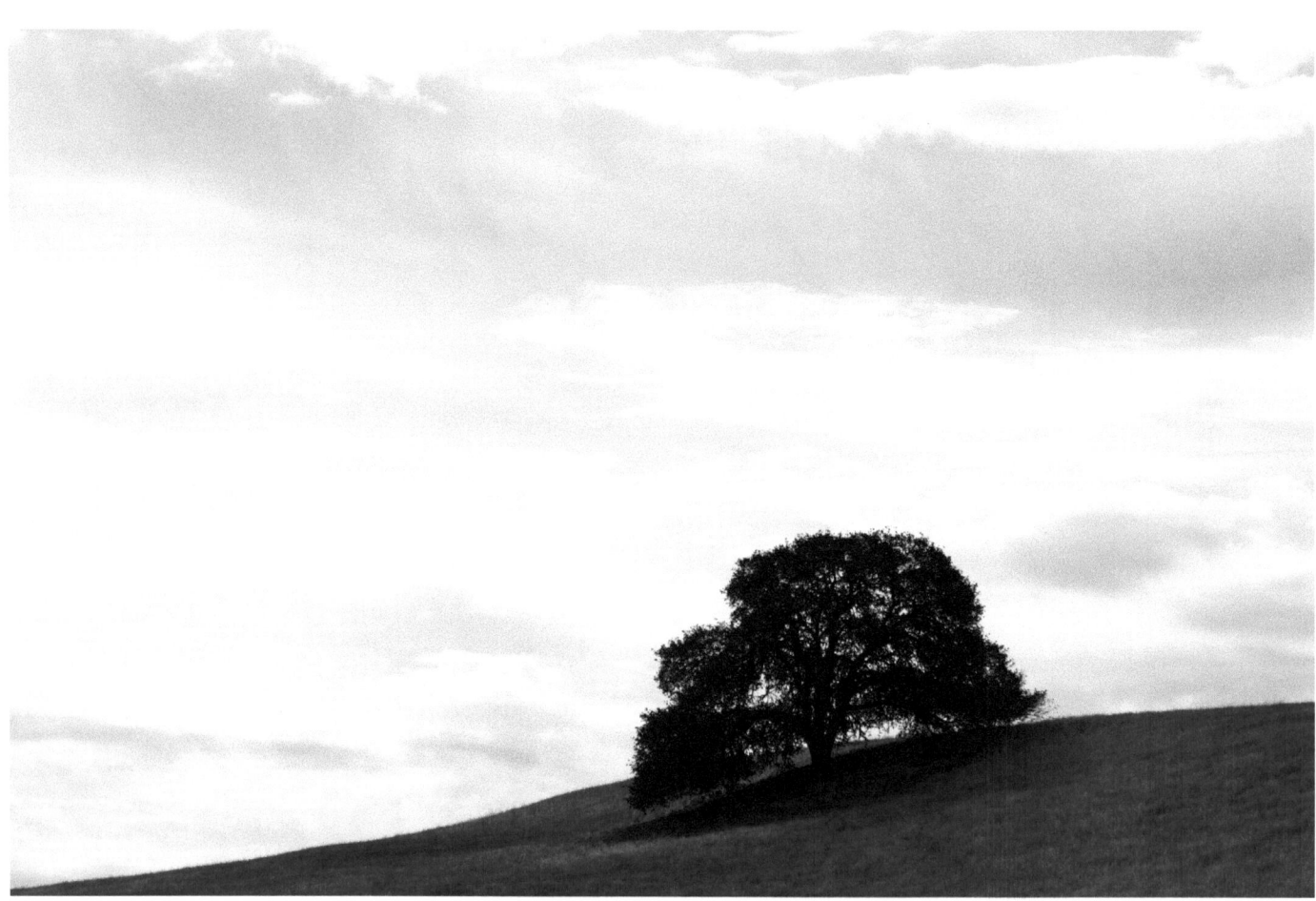

0531

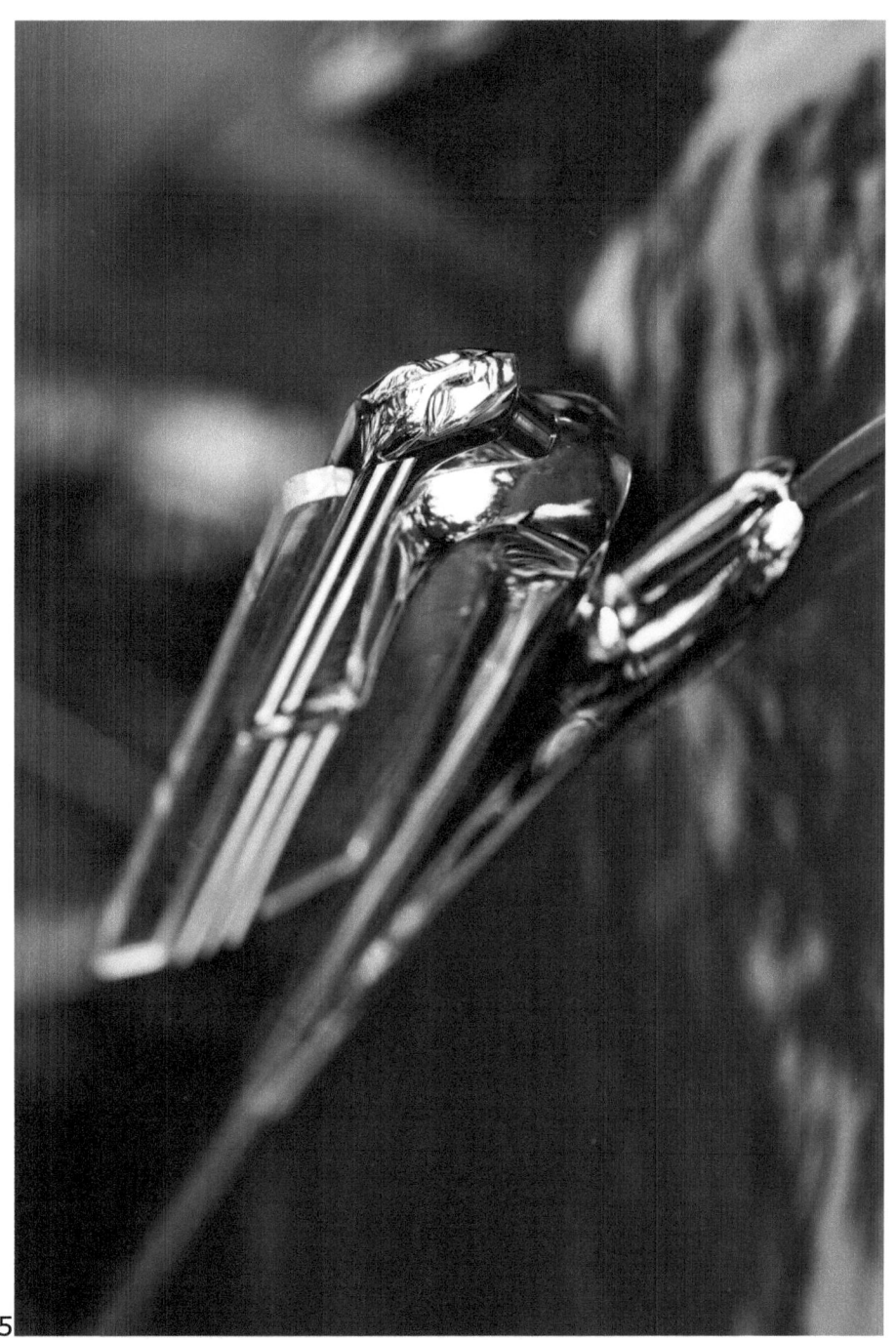

0705

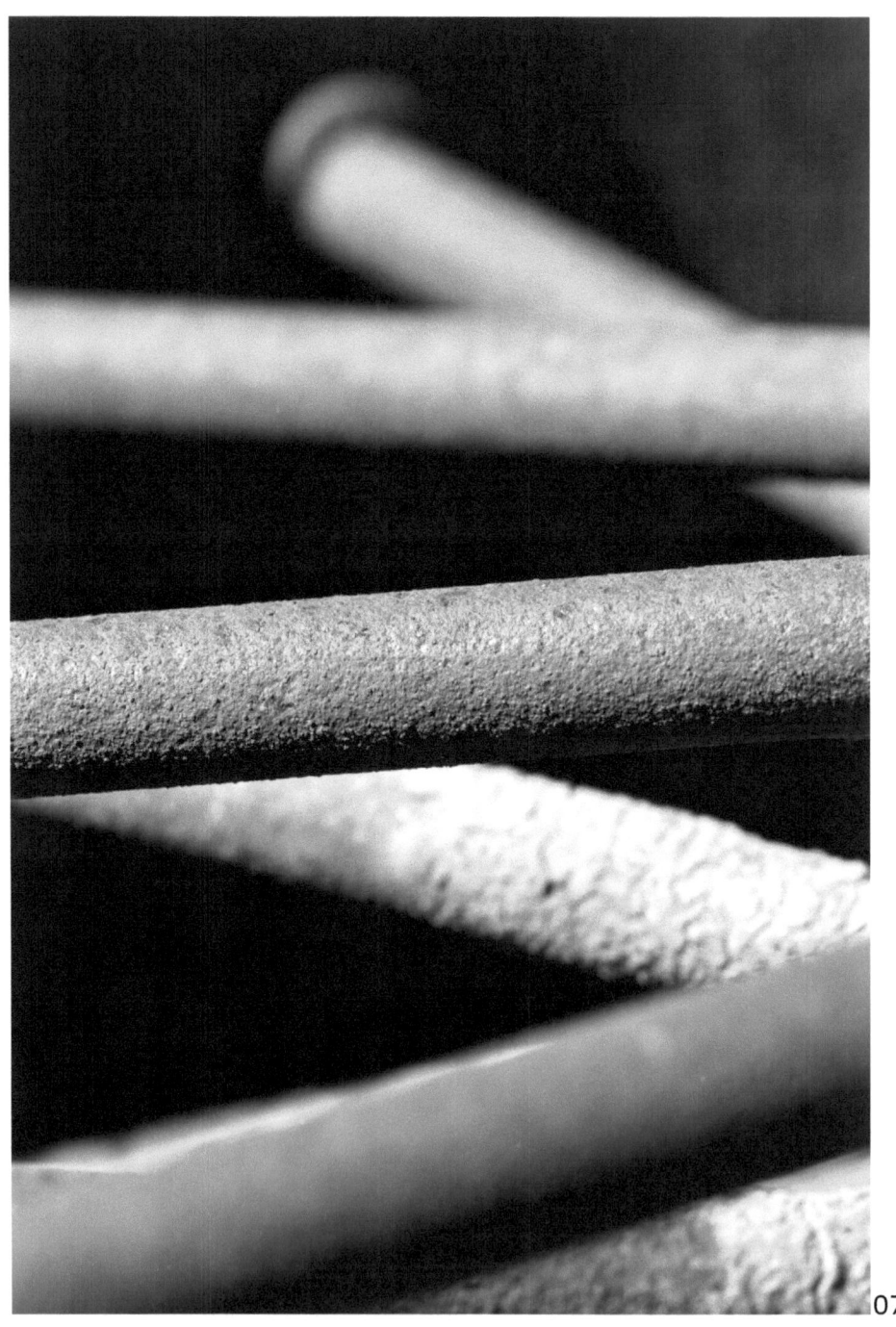

0780

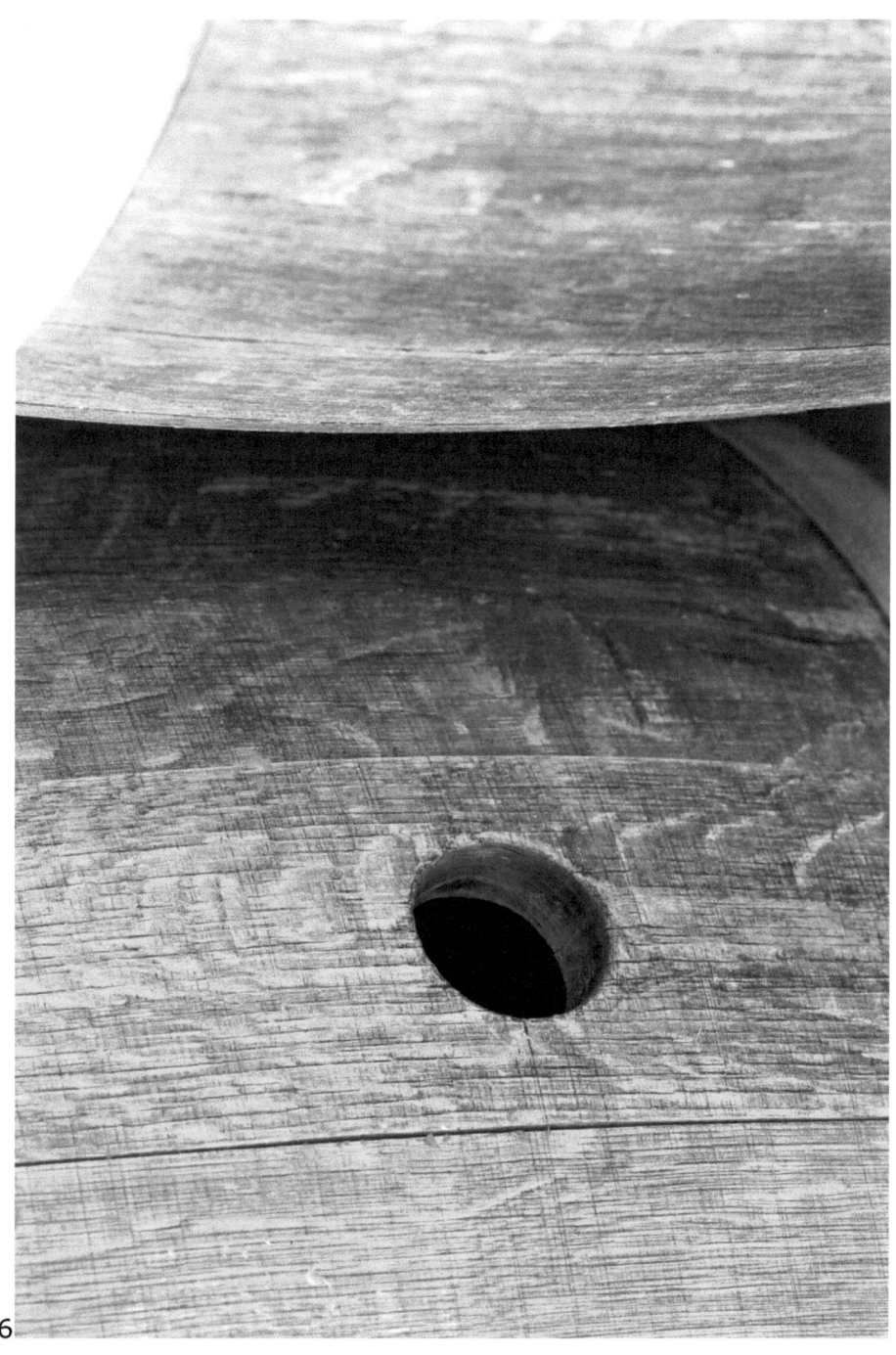

0826

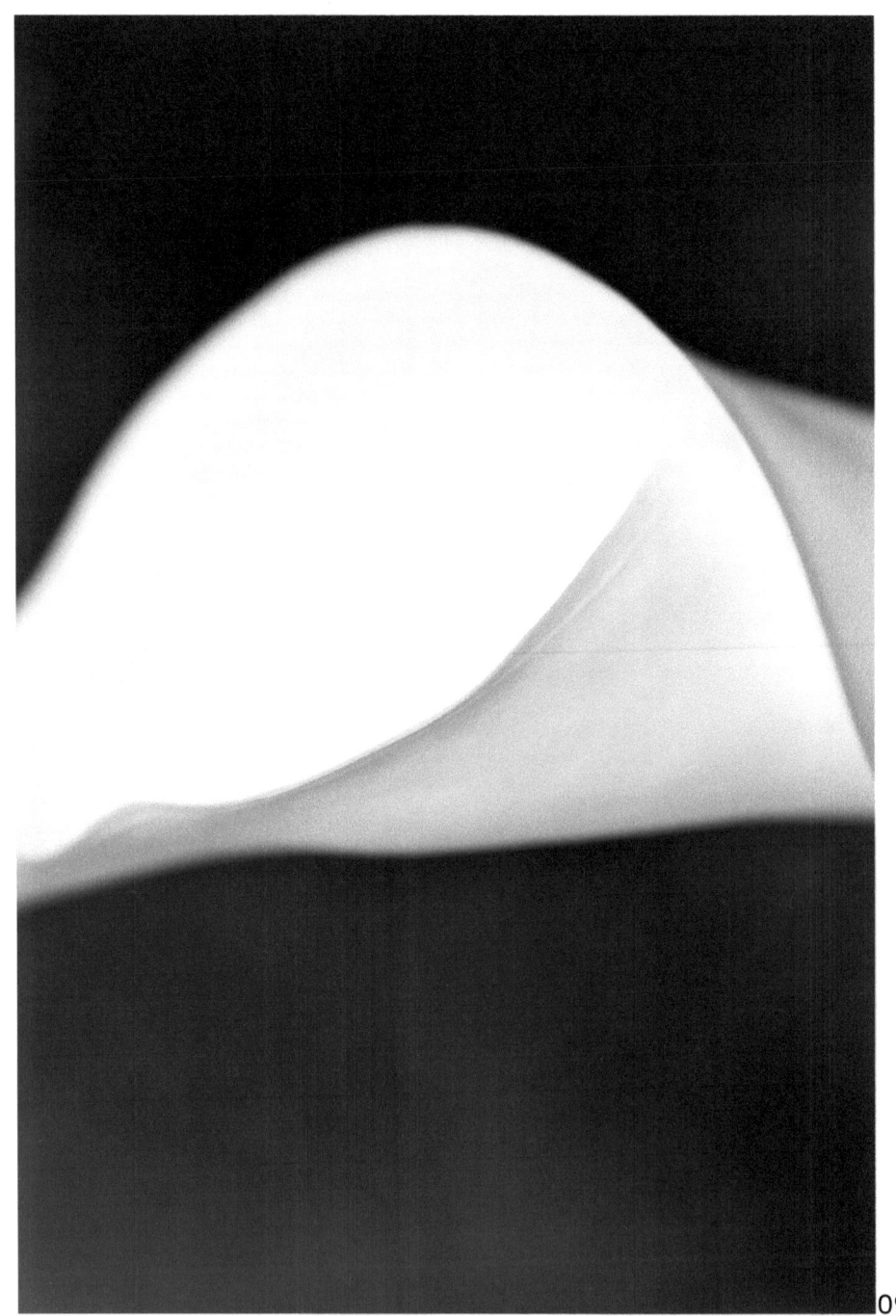

0920

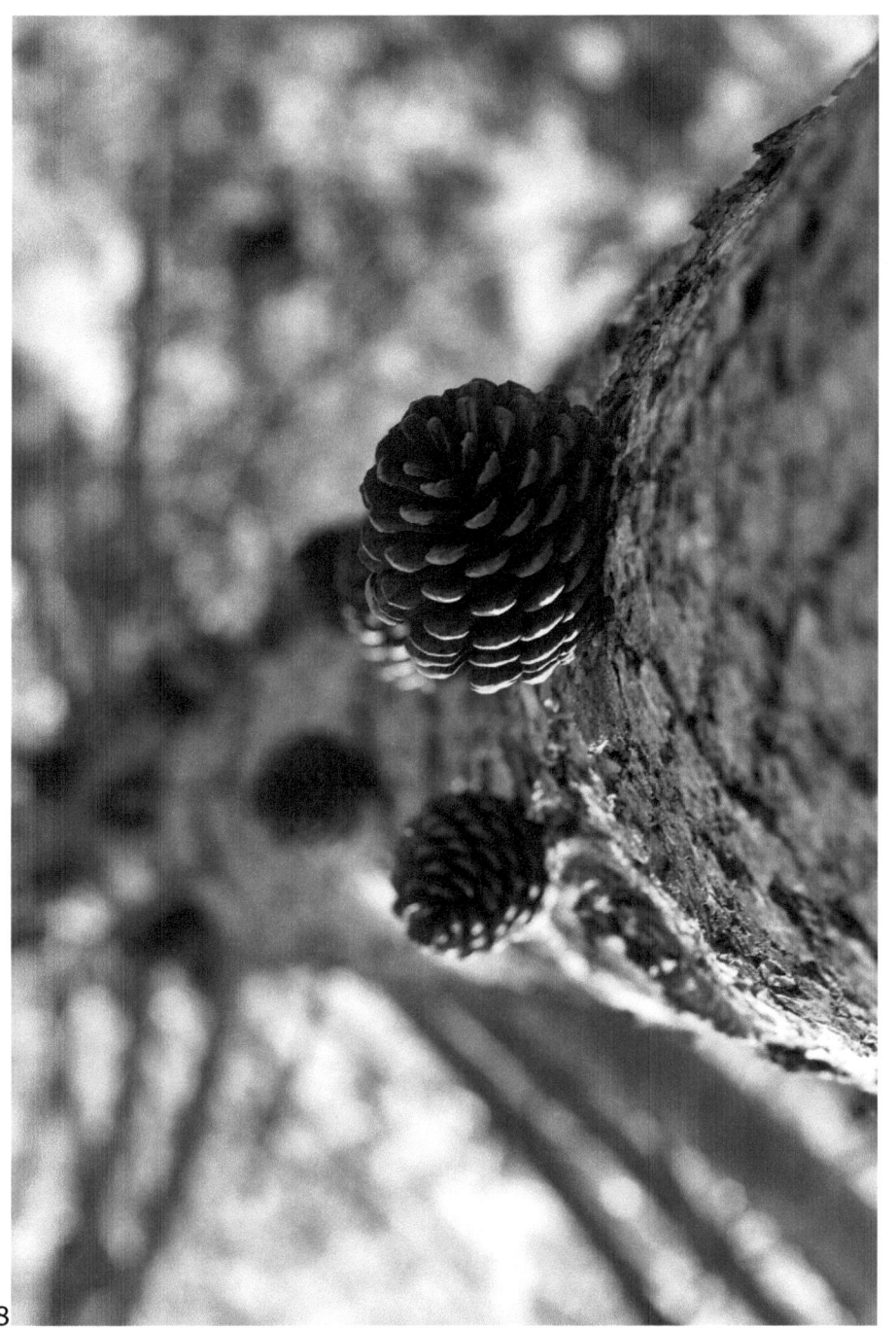

0938

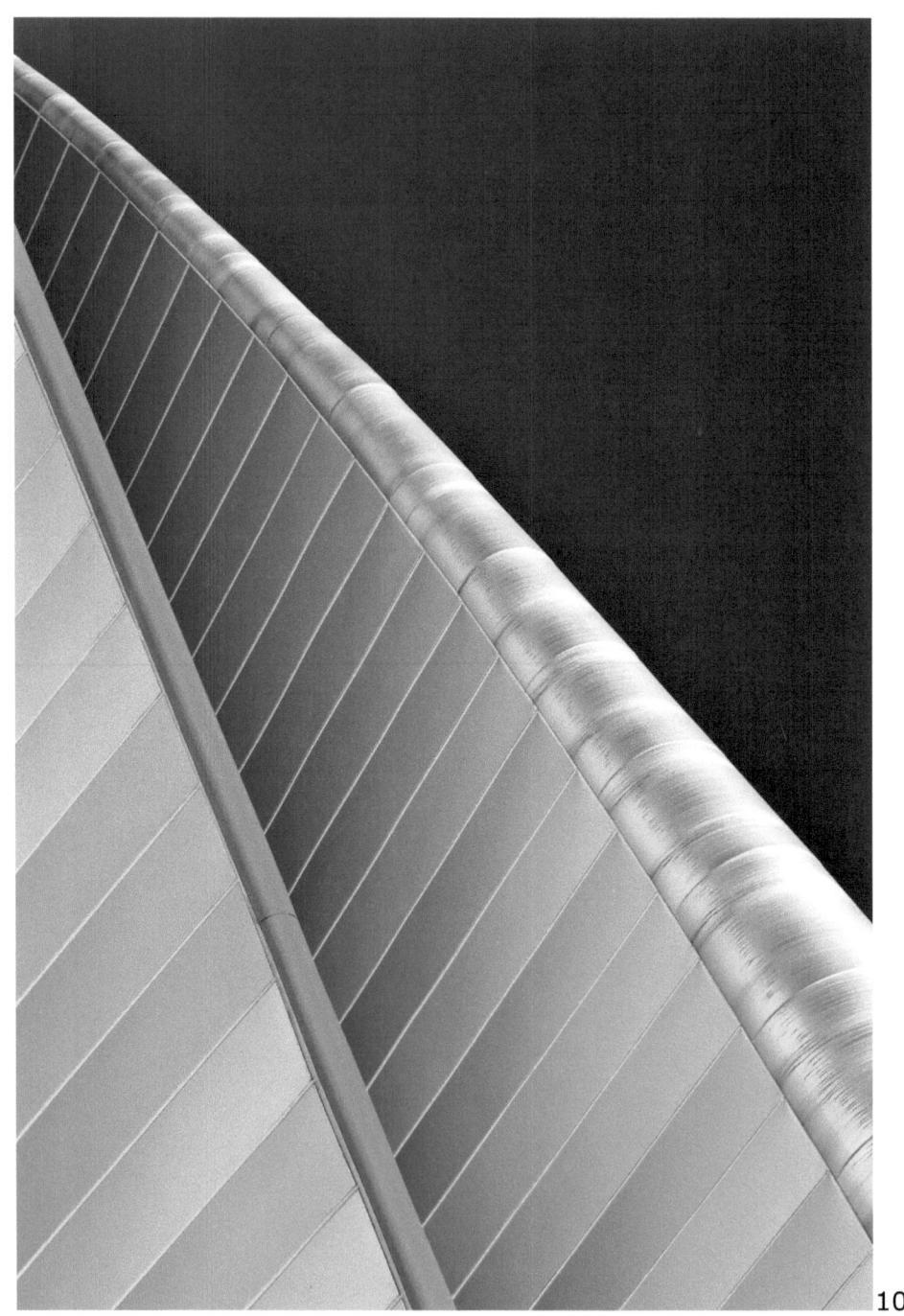

1096

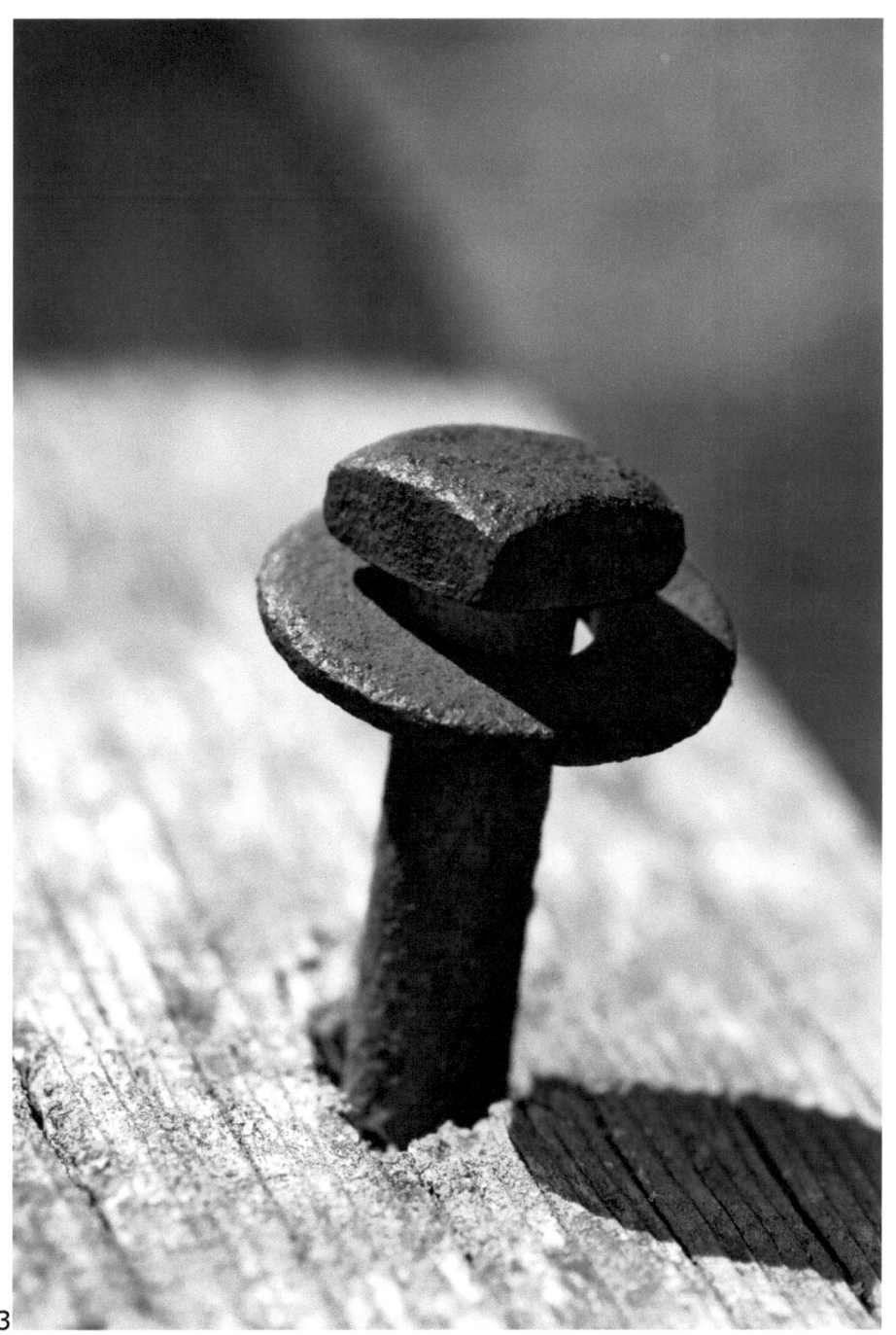

1173

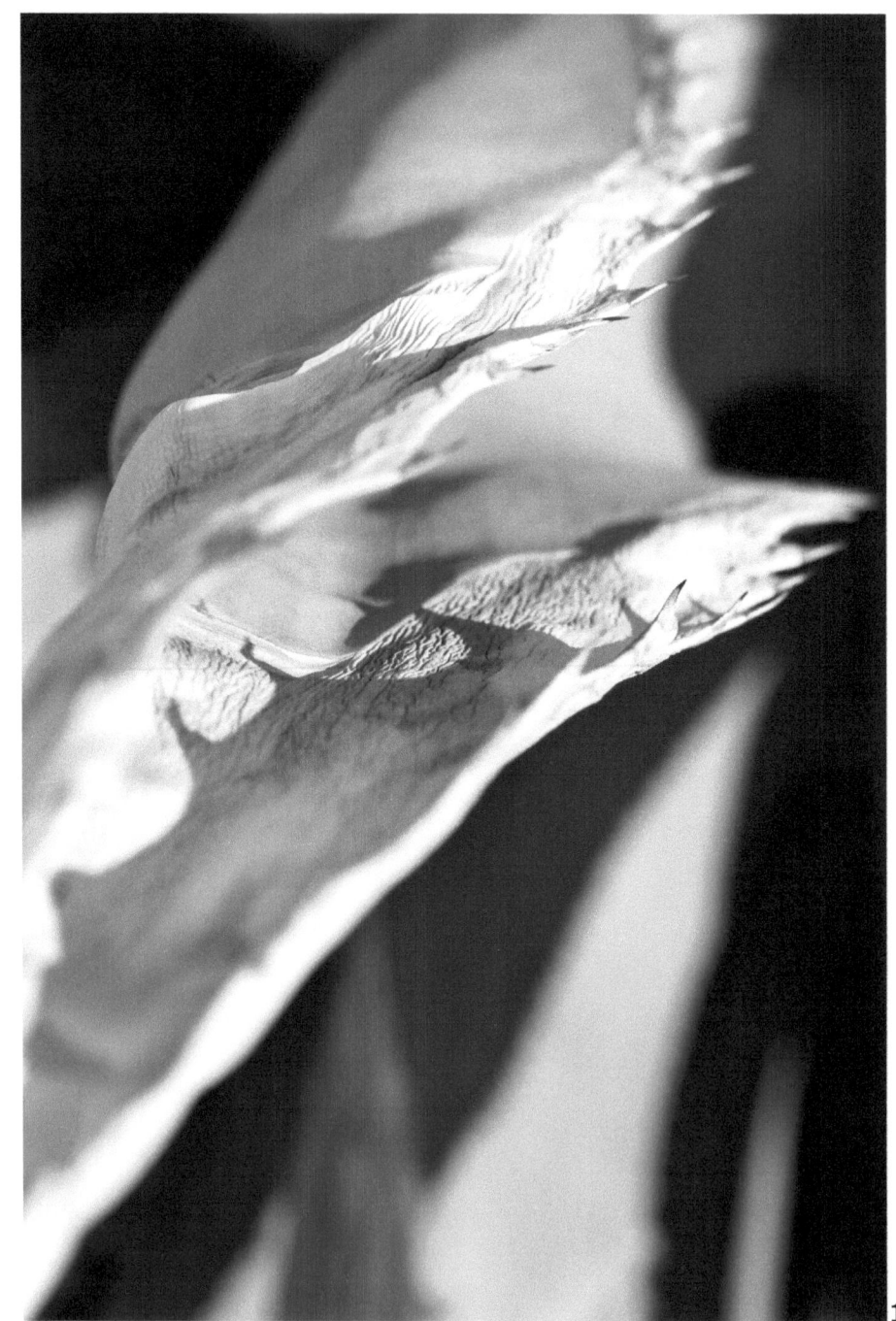

1581

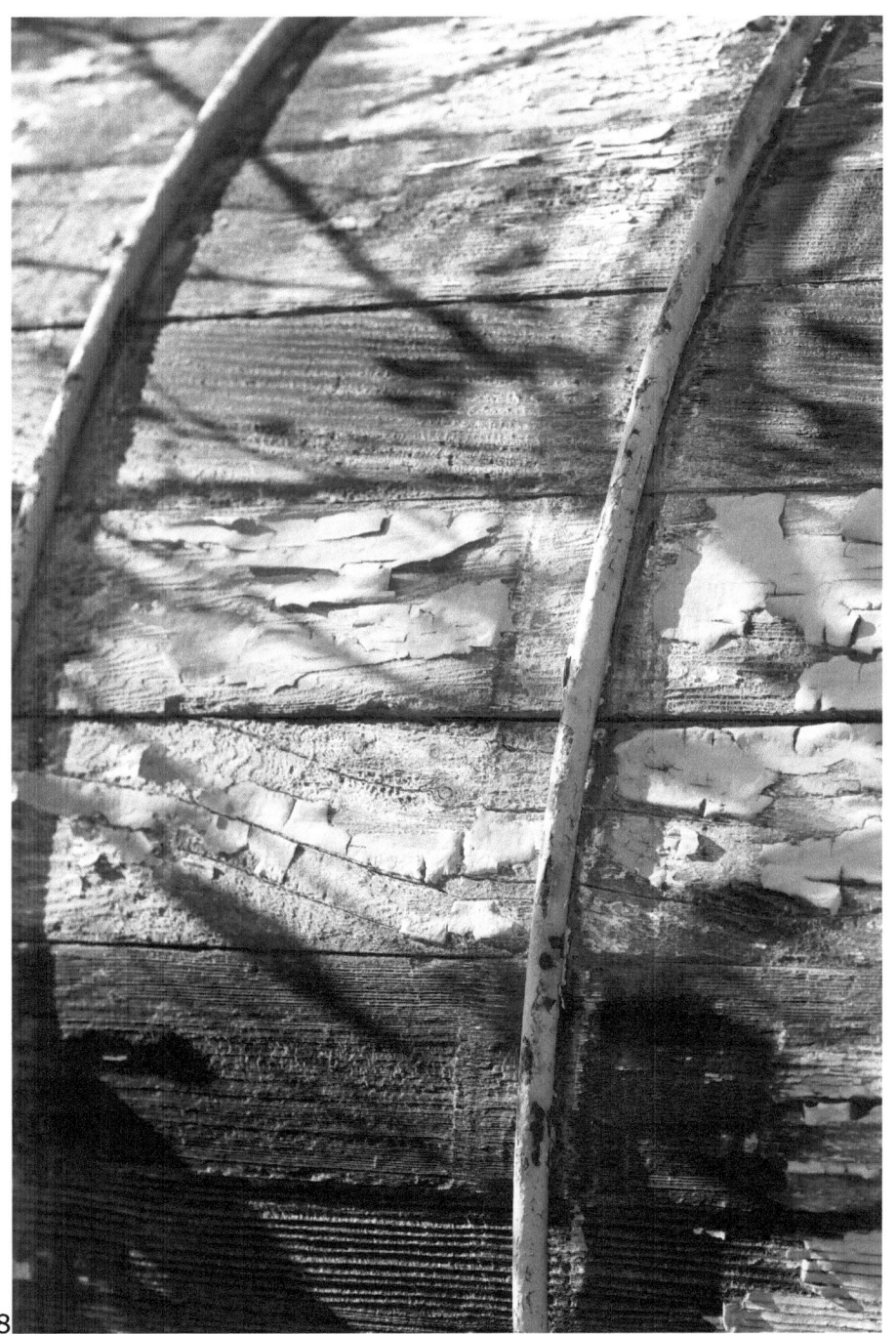

1608

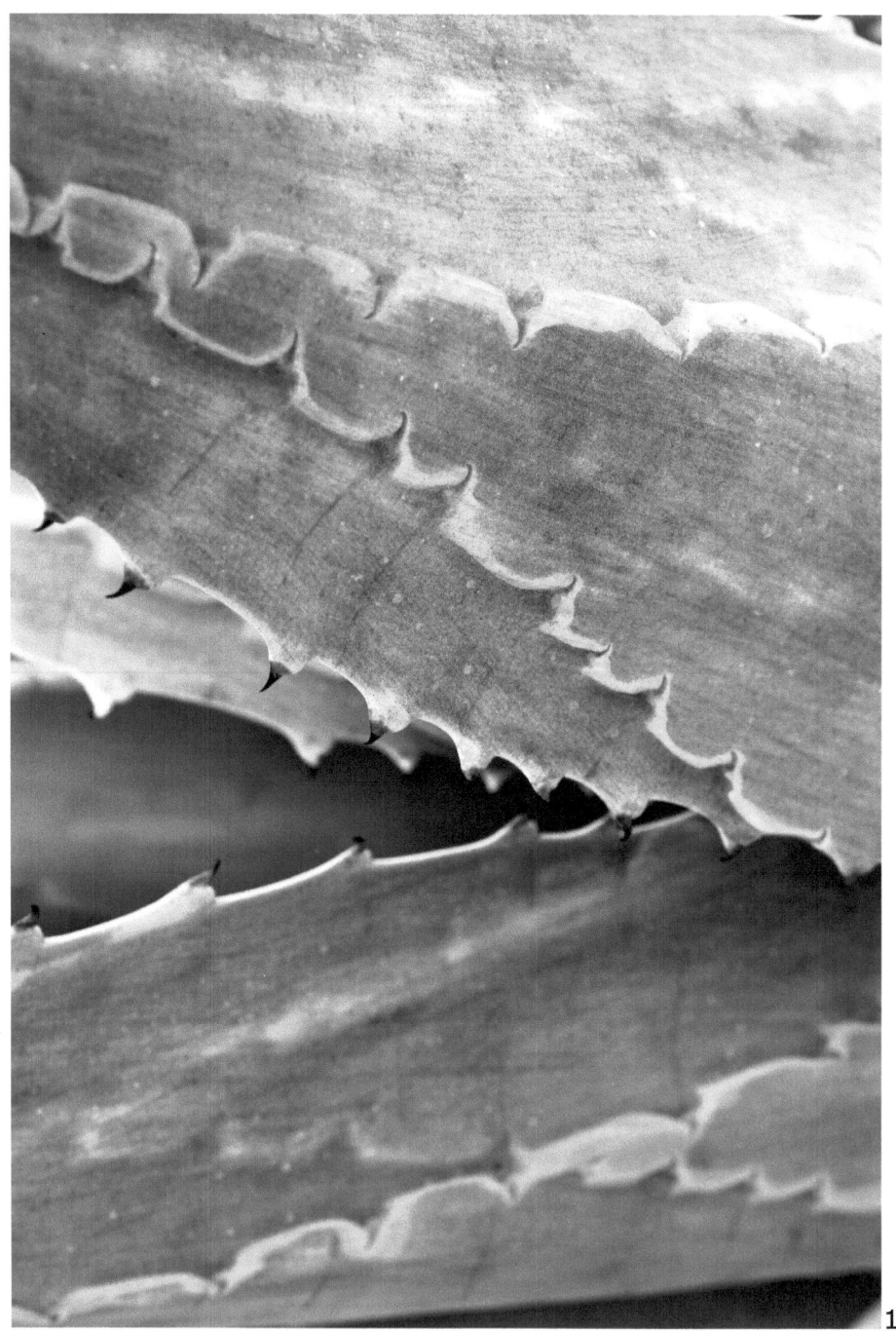

1976

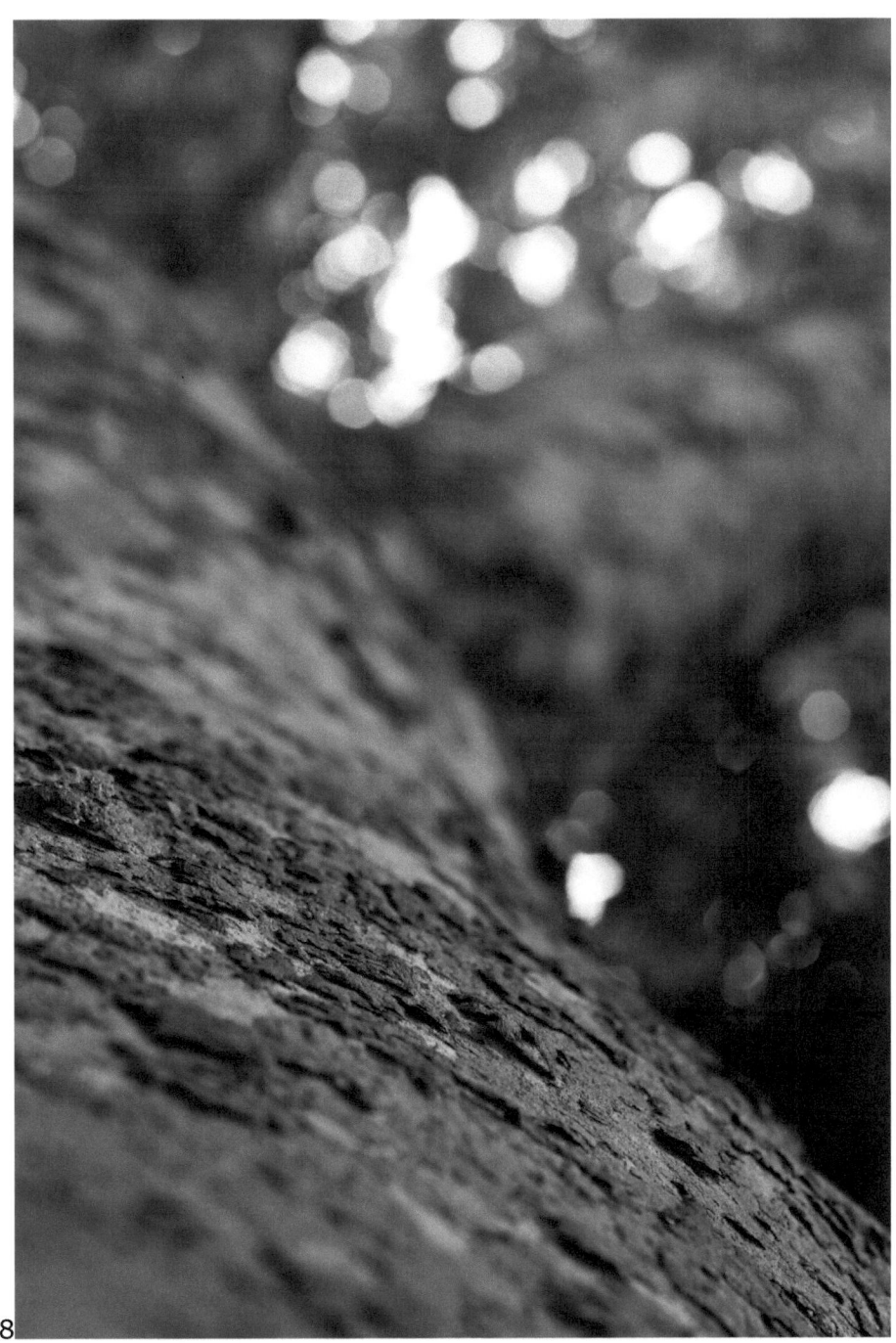

2068

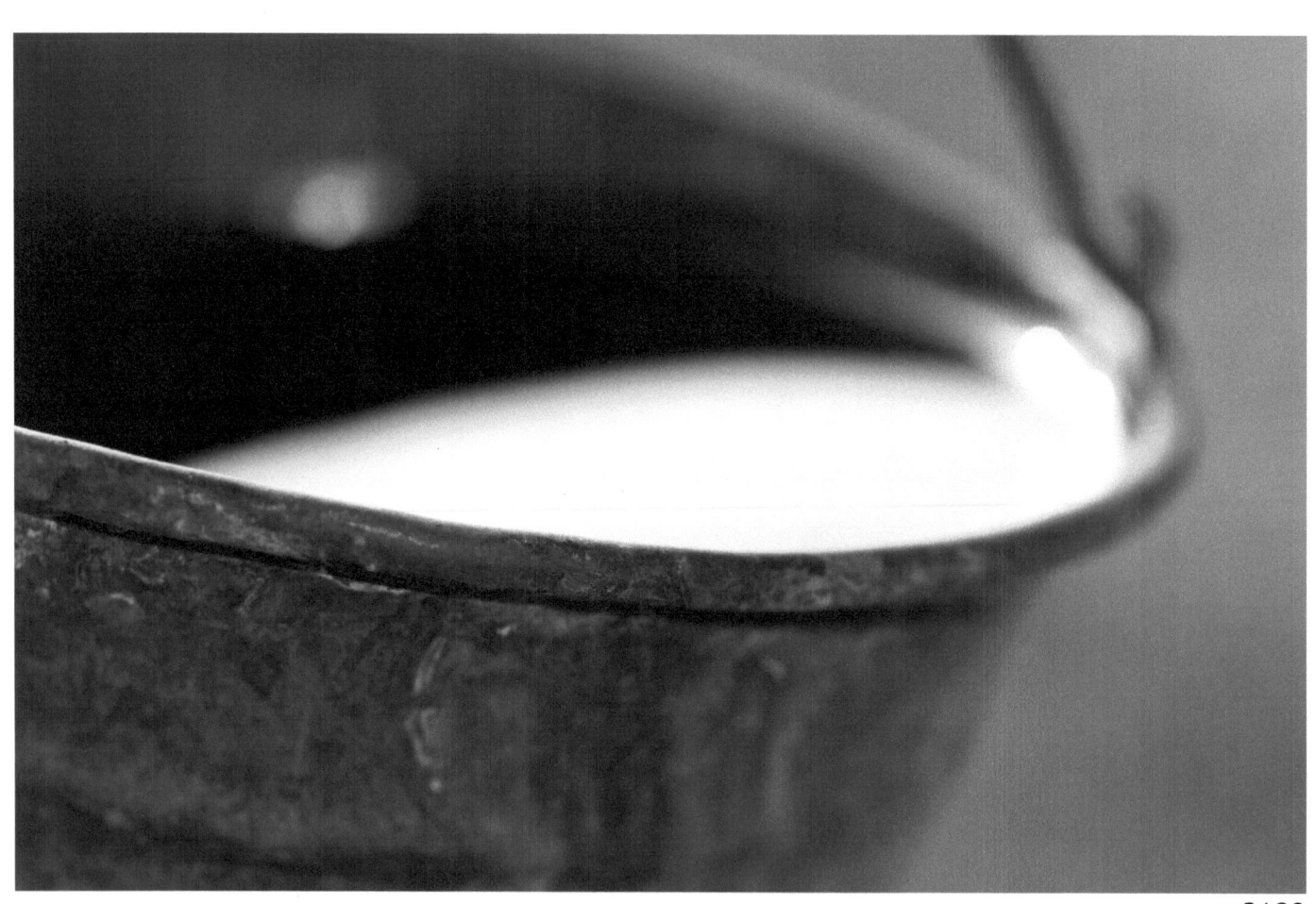

2180

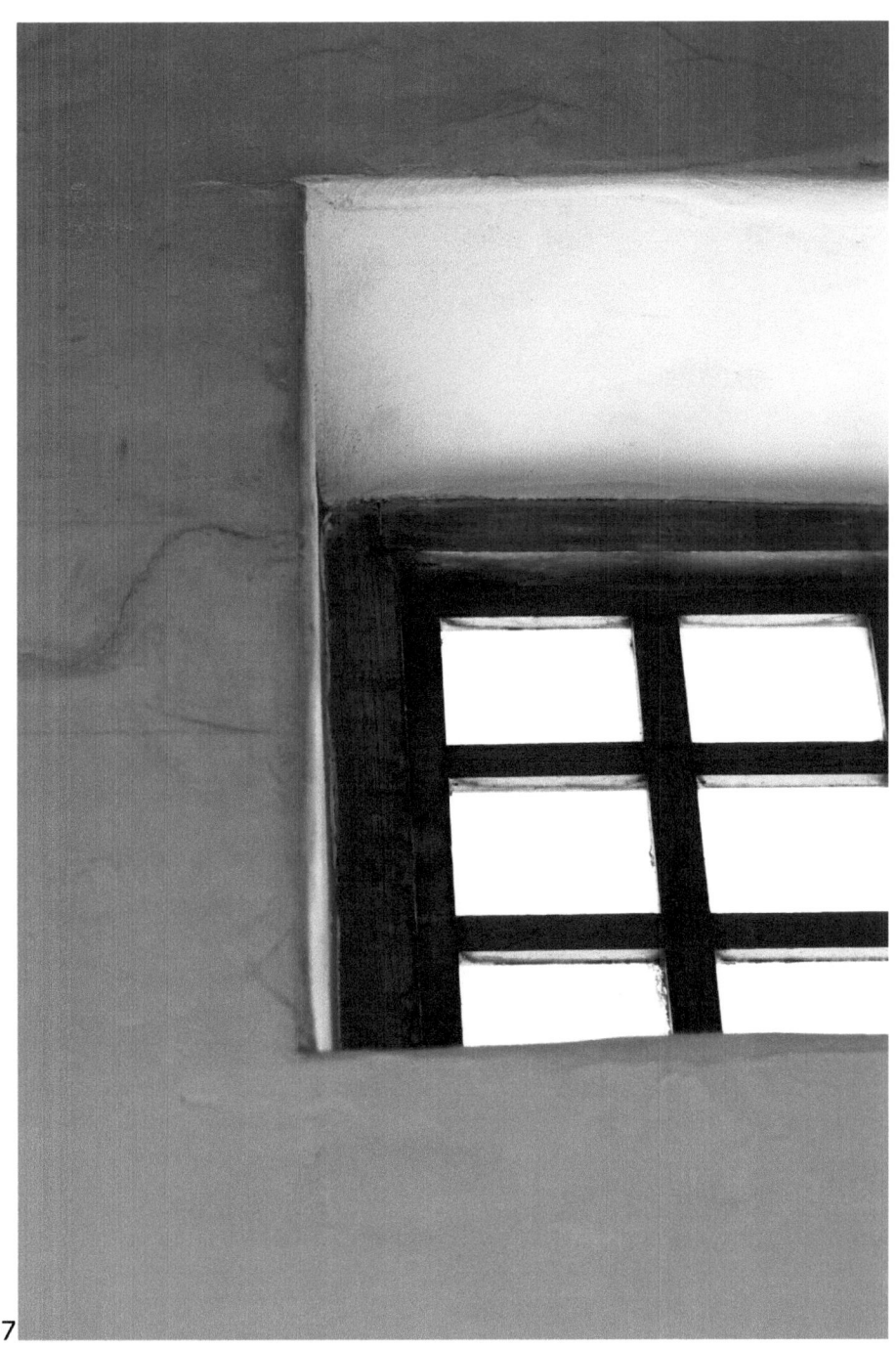

2397

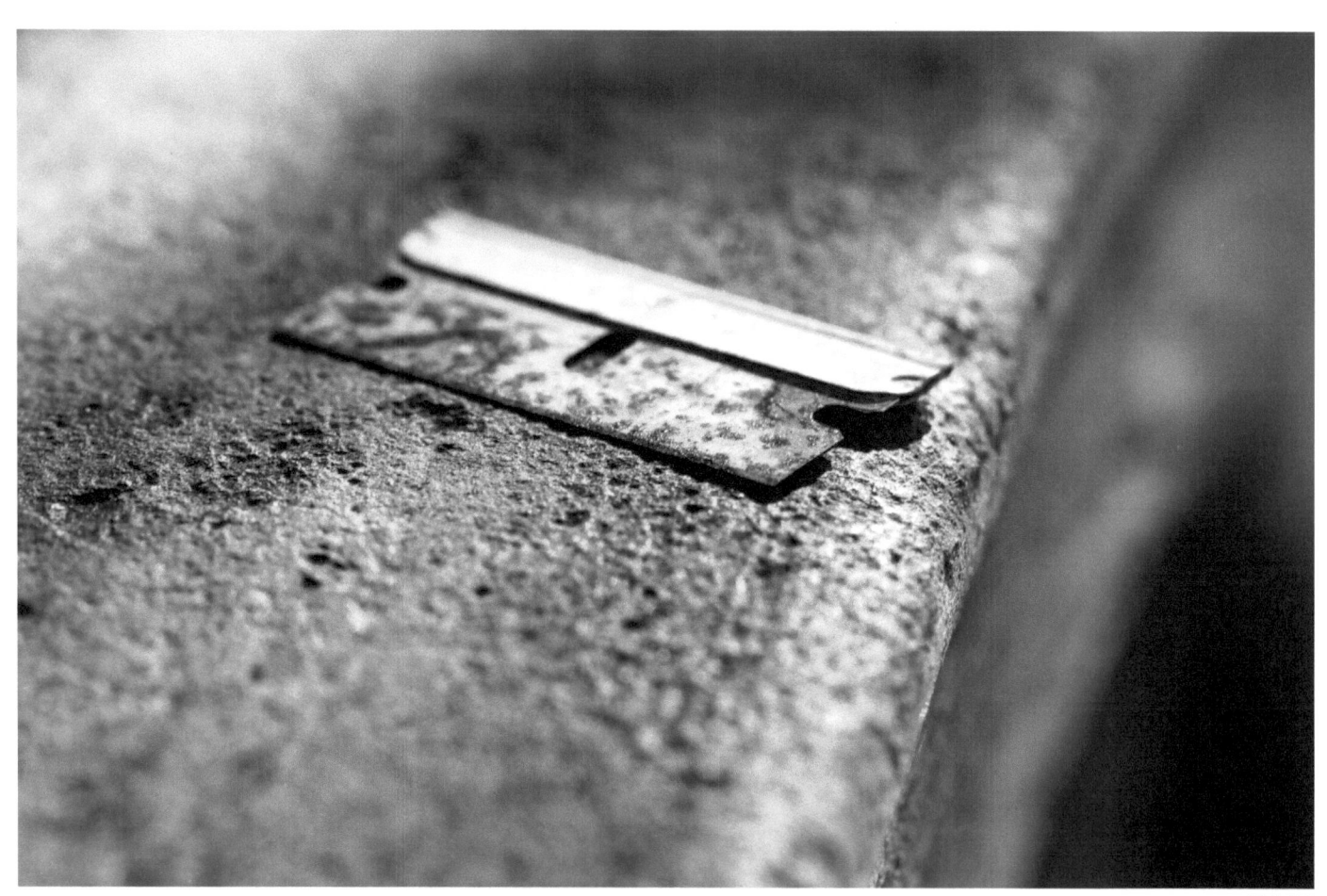

2467

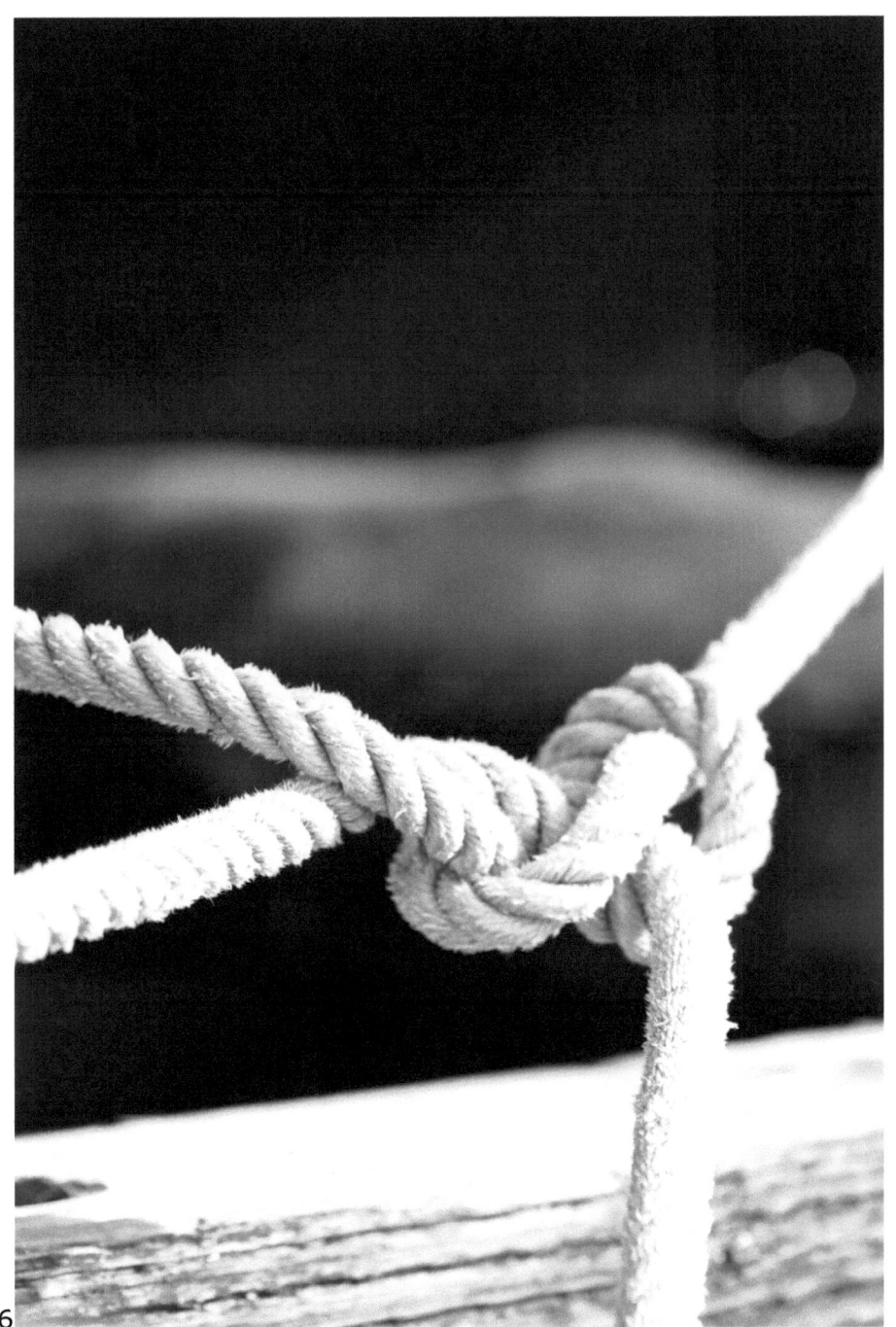

2686

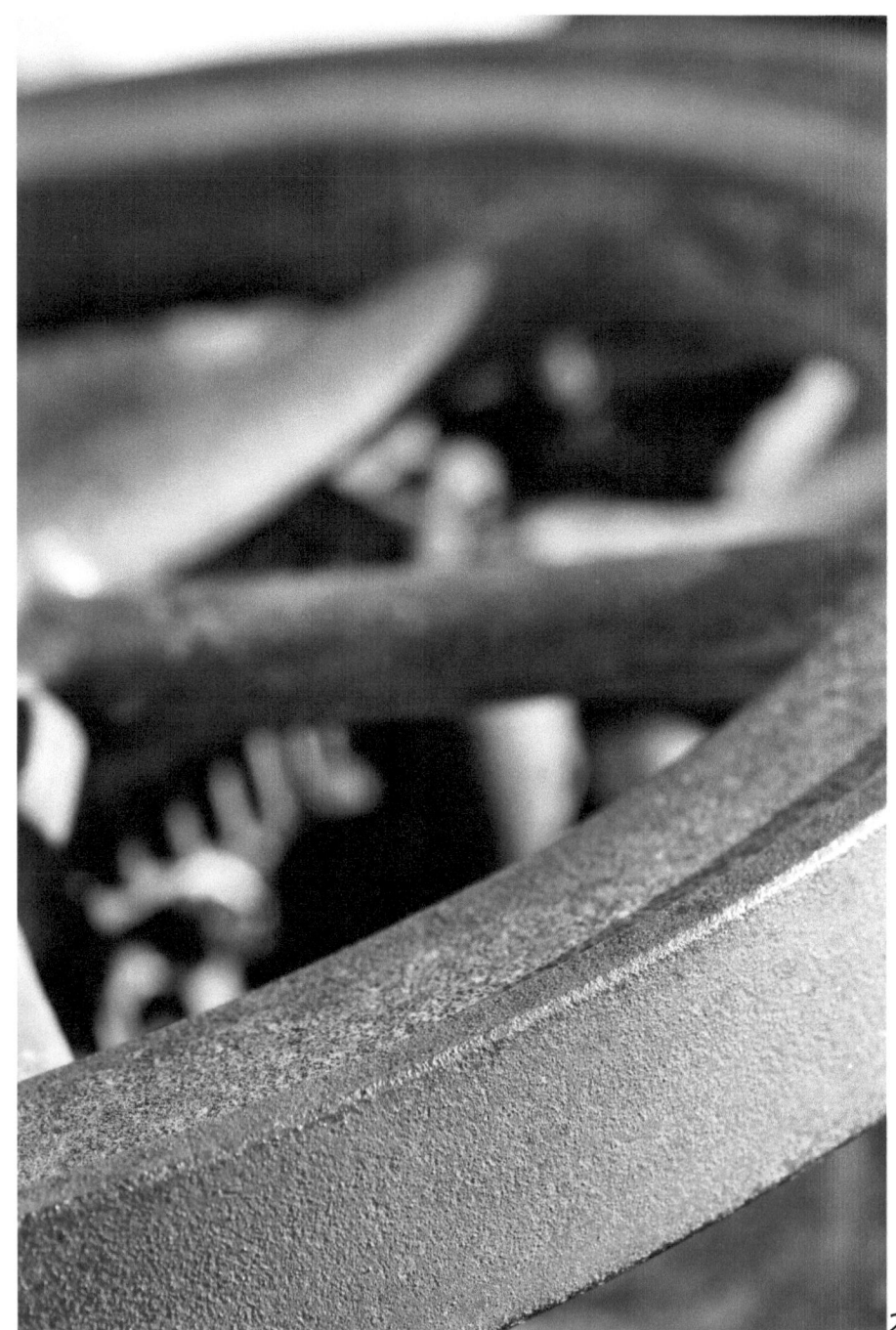

2962

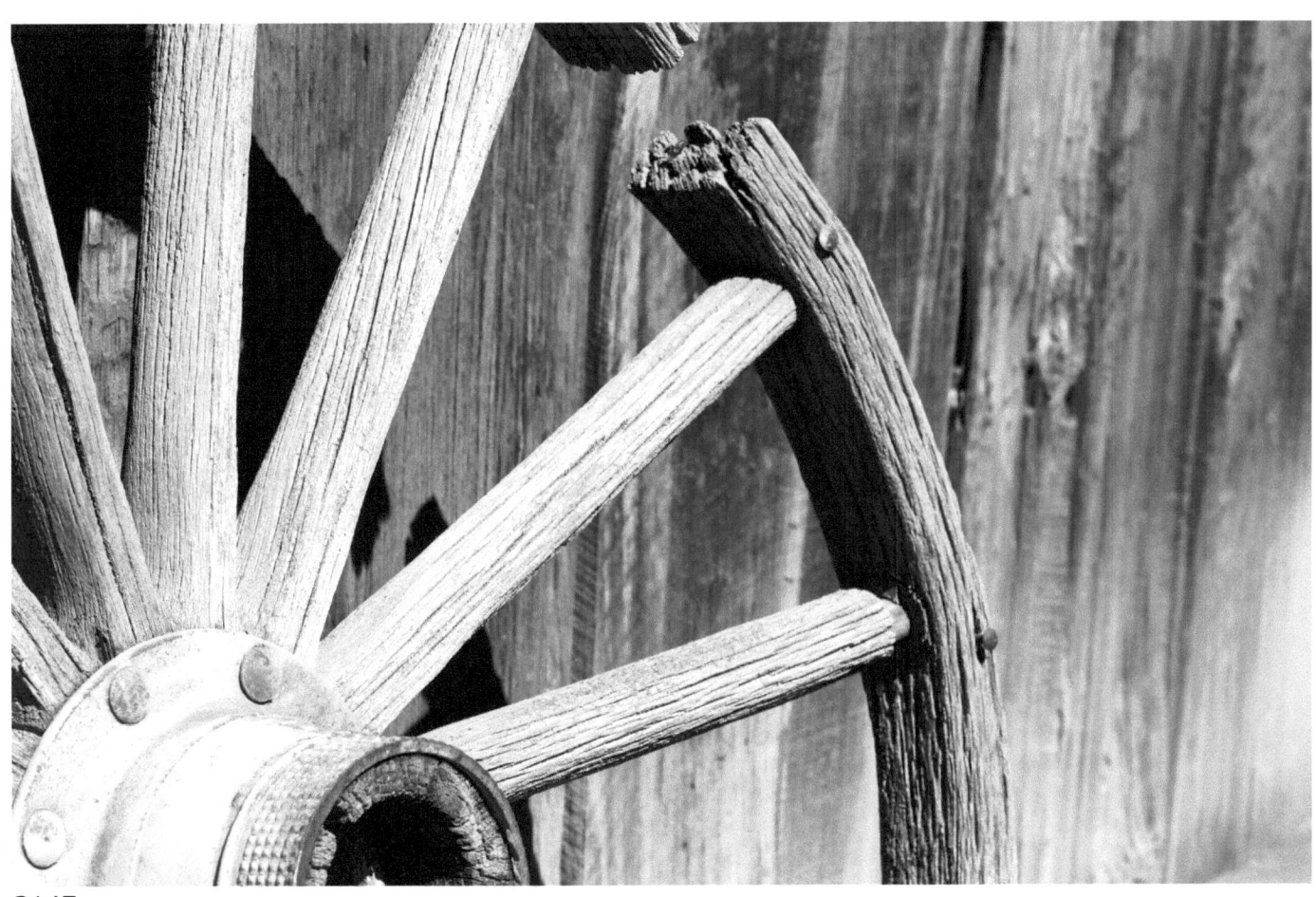

3147

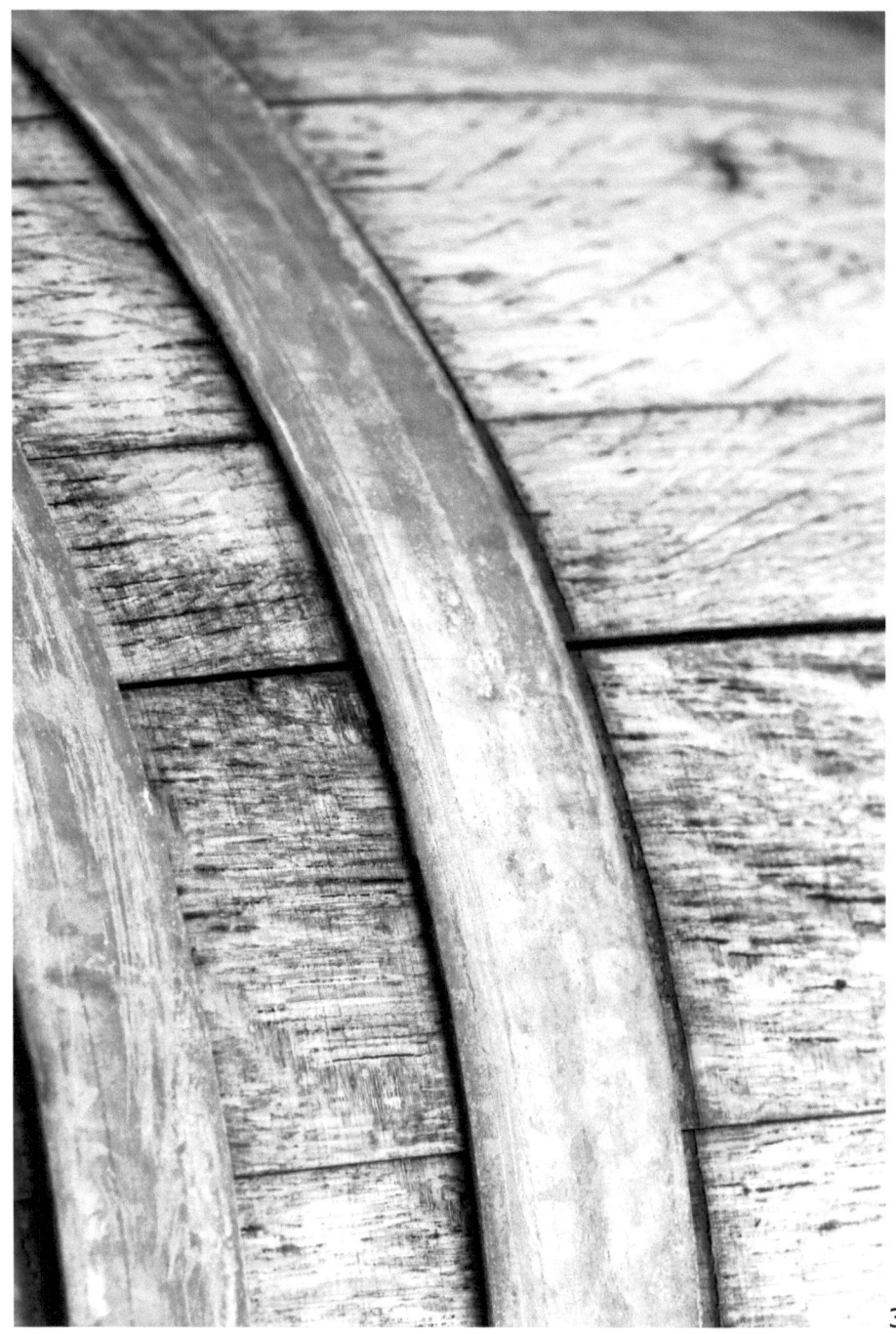

3151

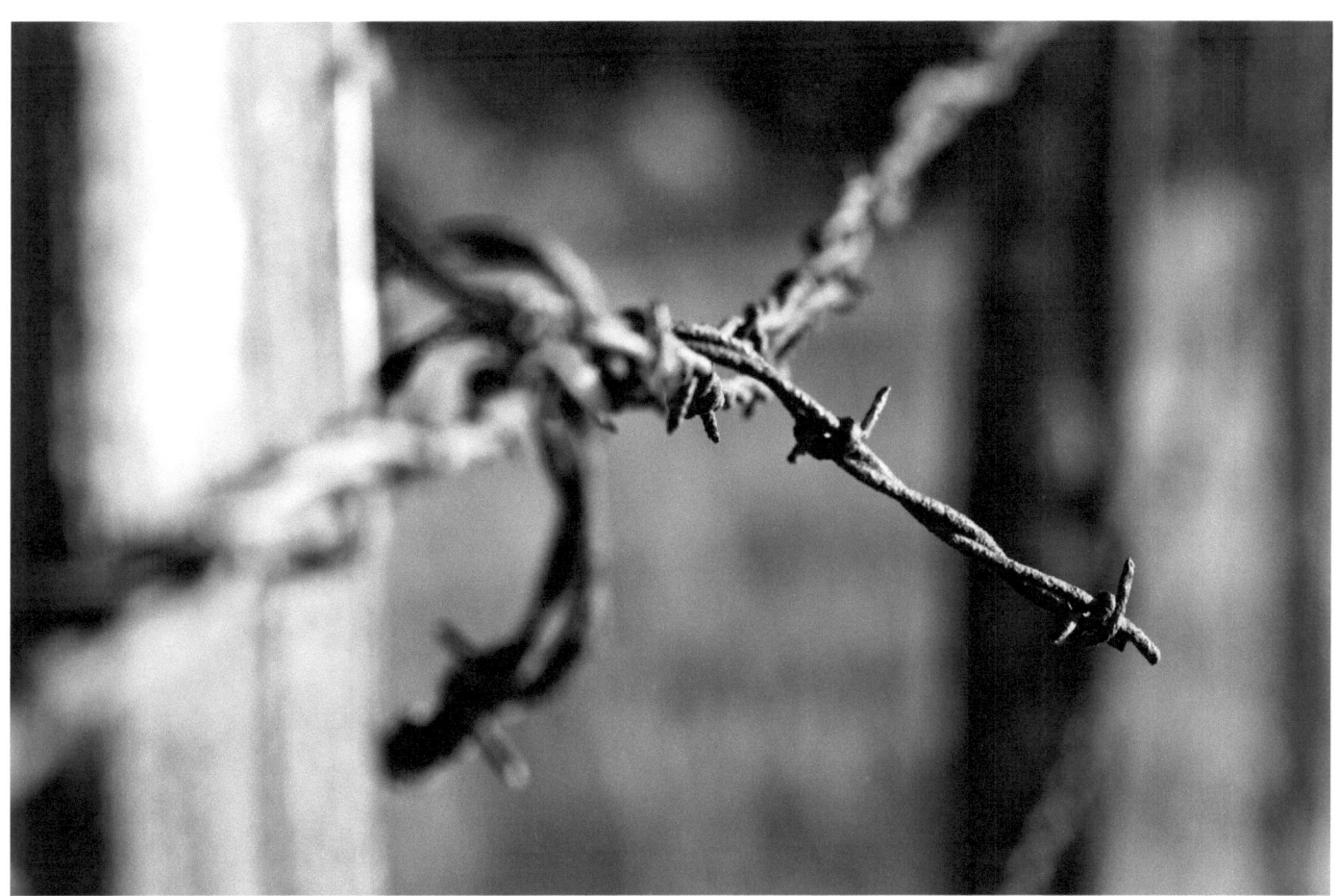

3359

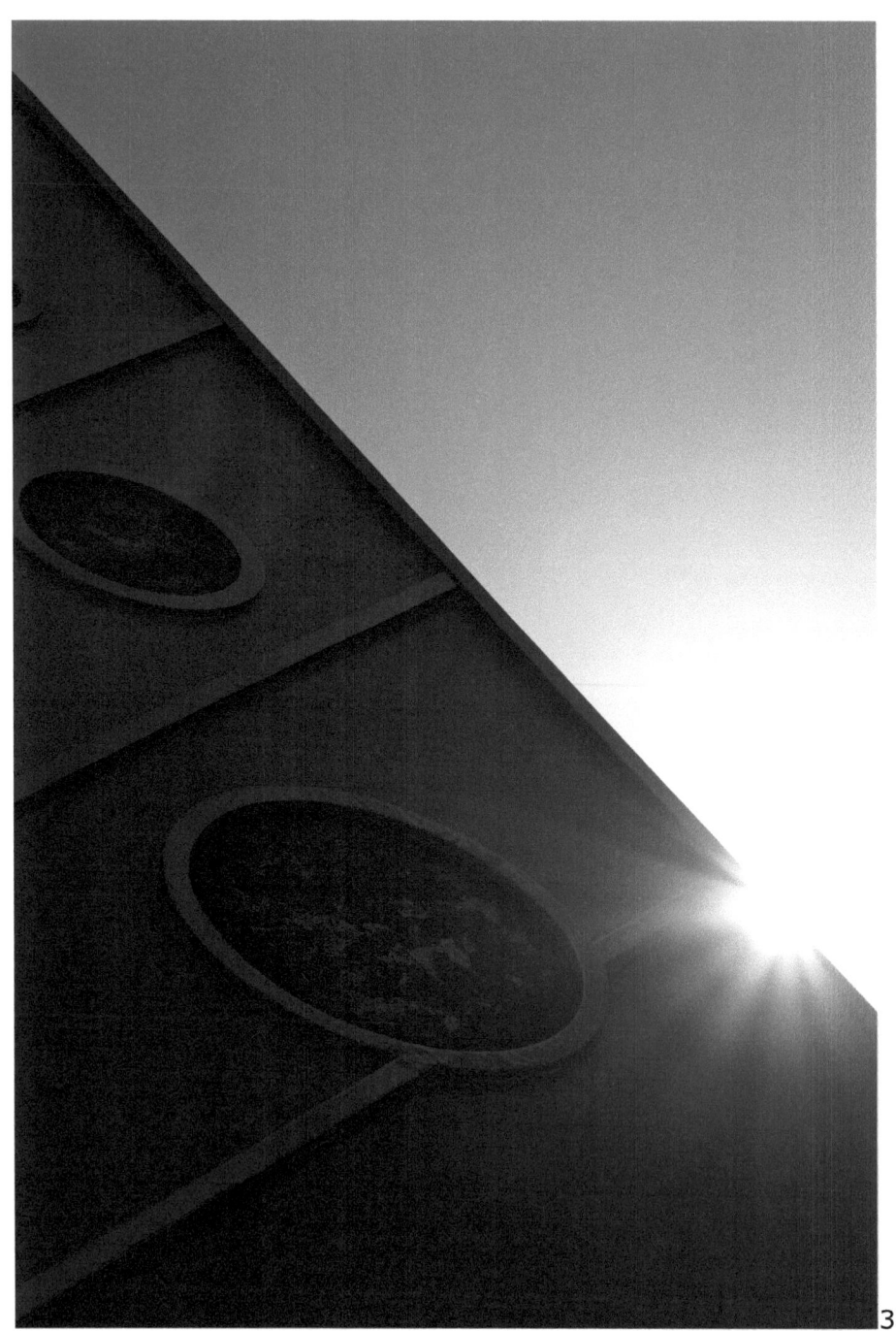

3621

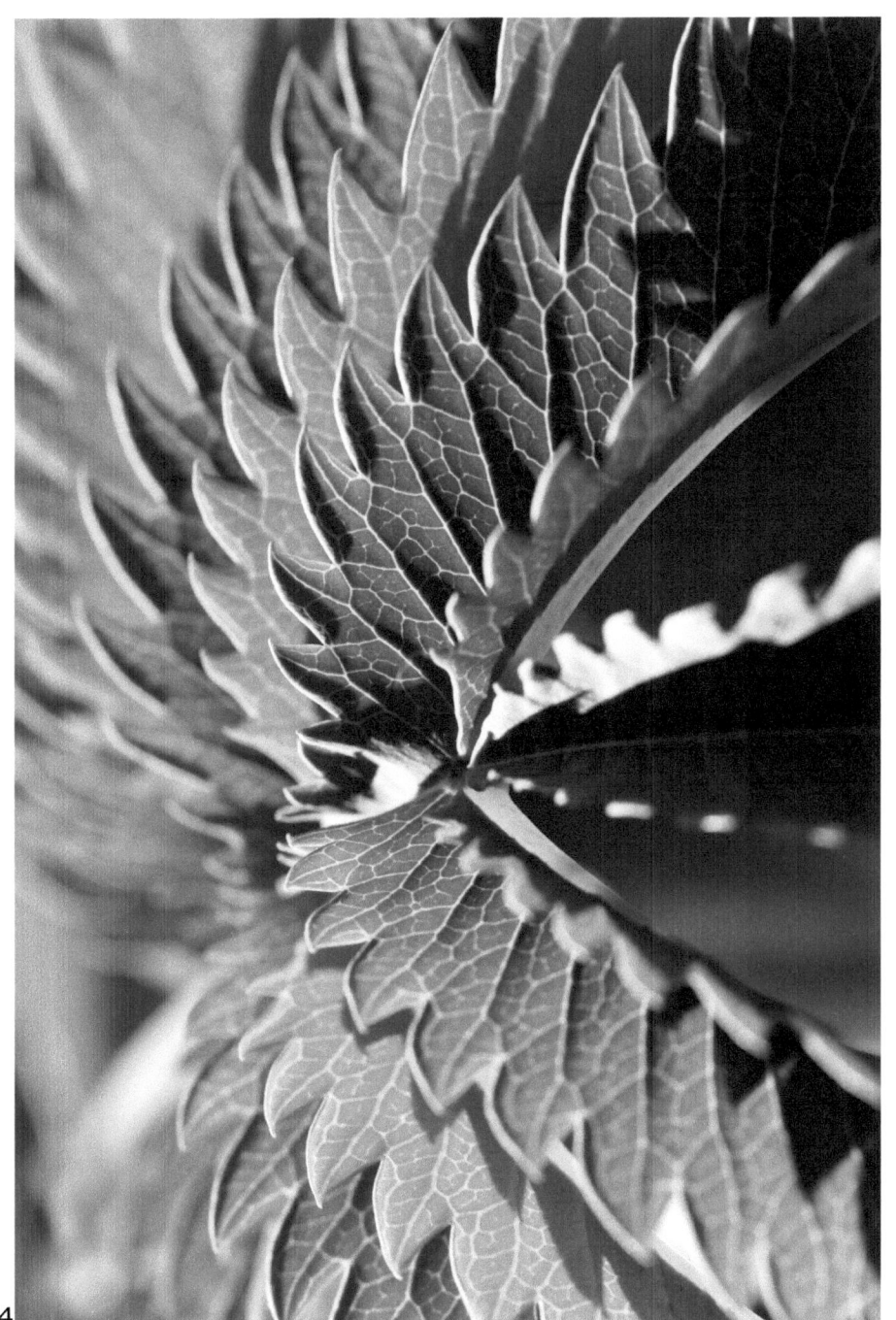

3714

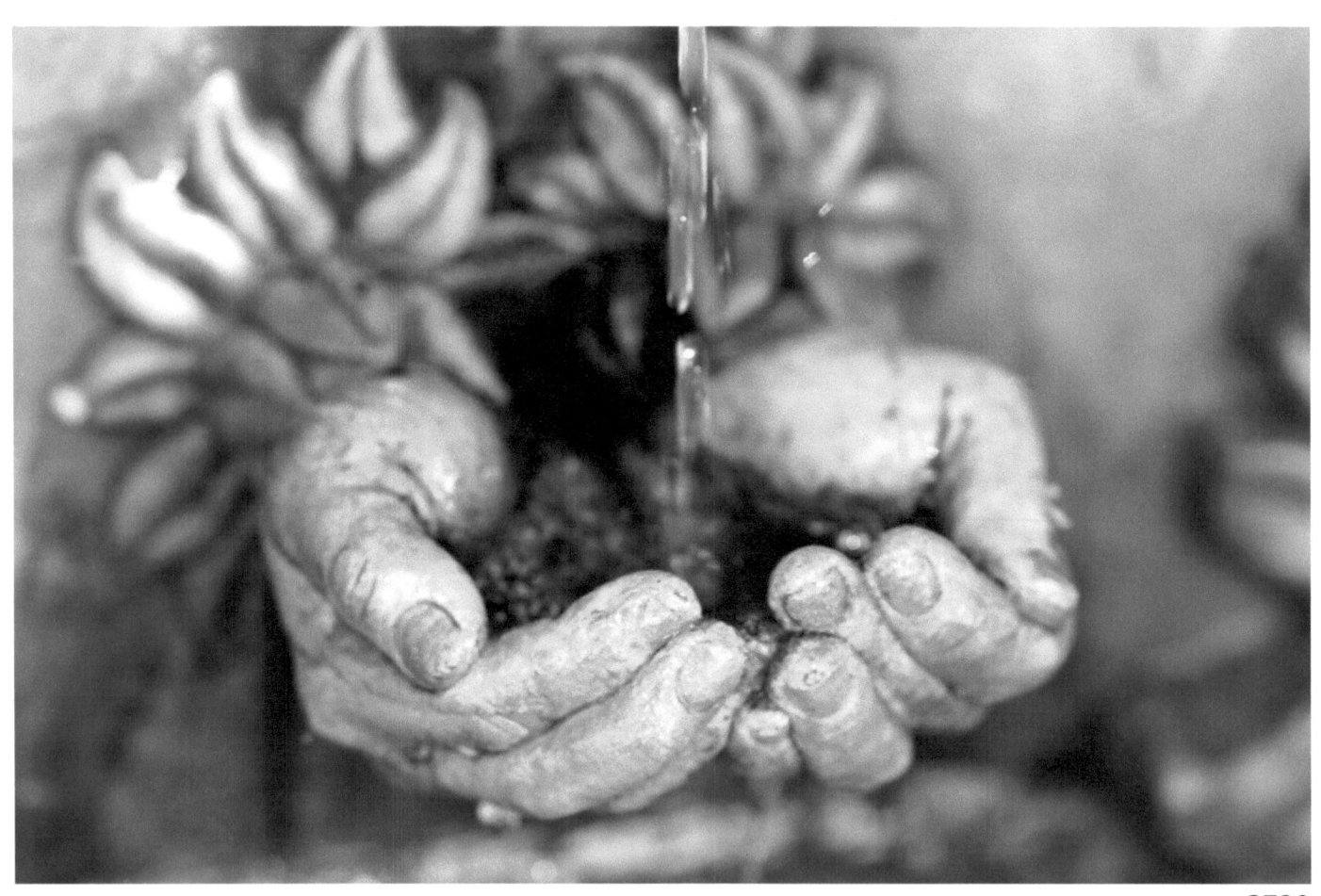

3720

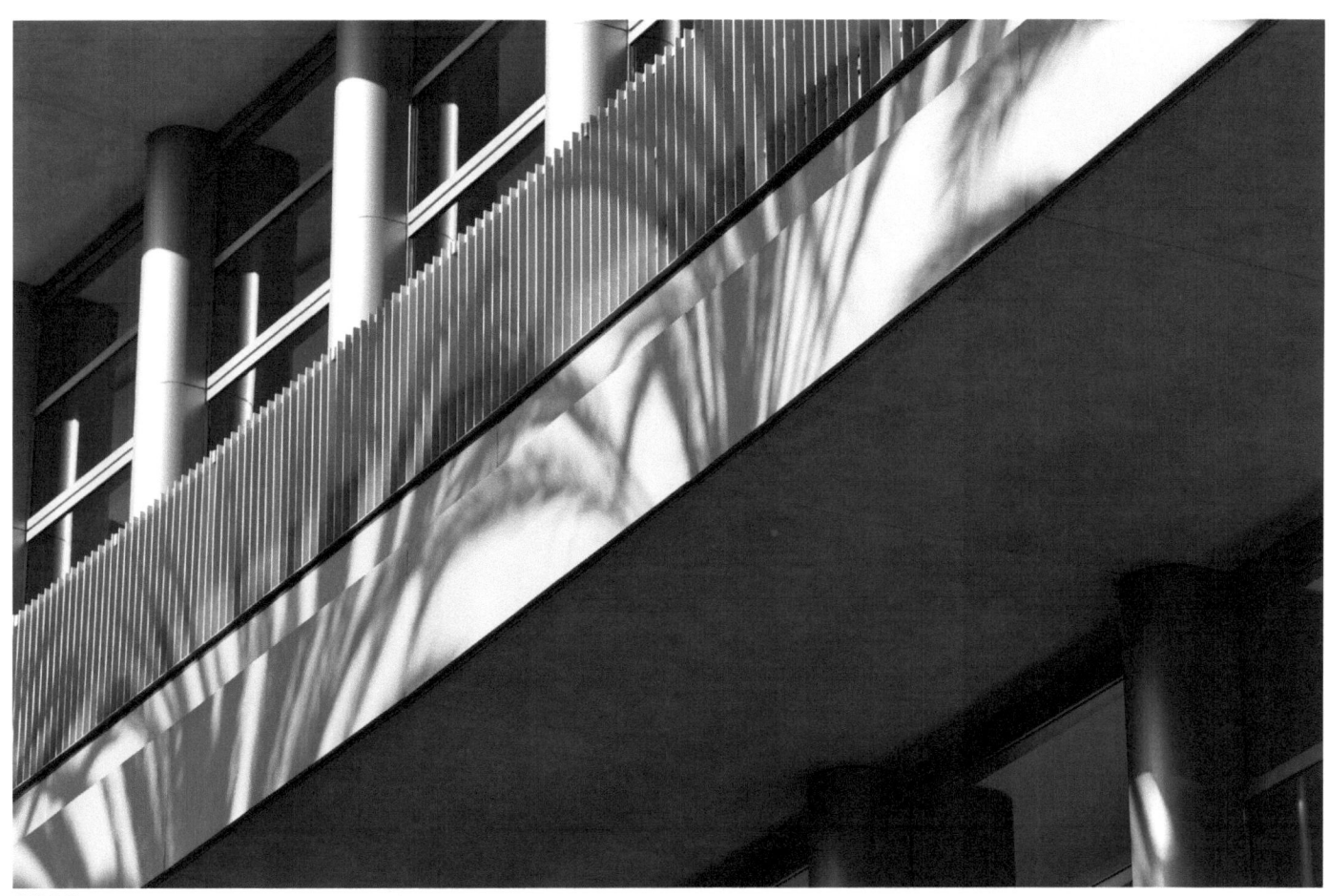

3916

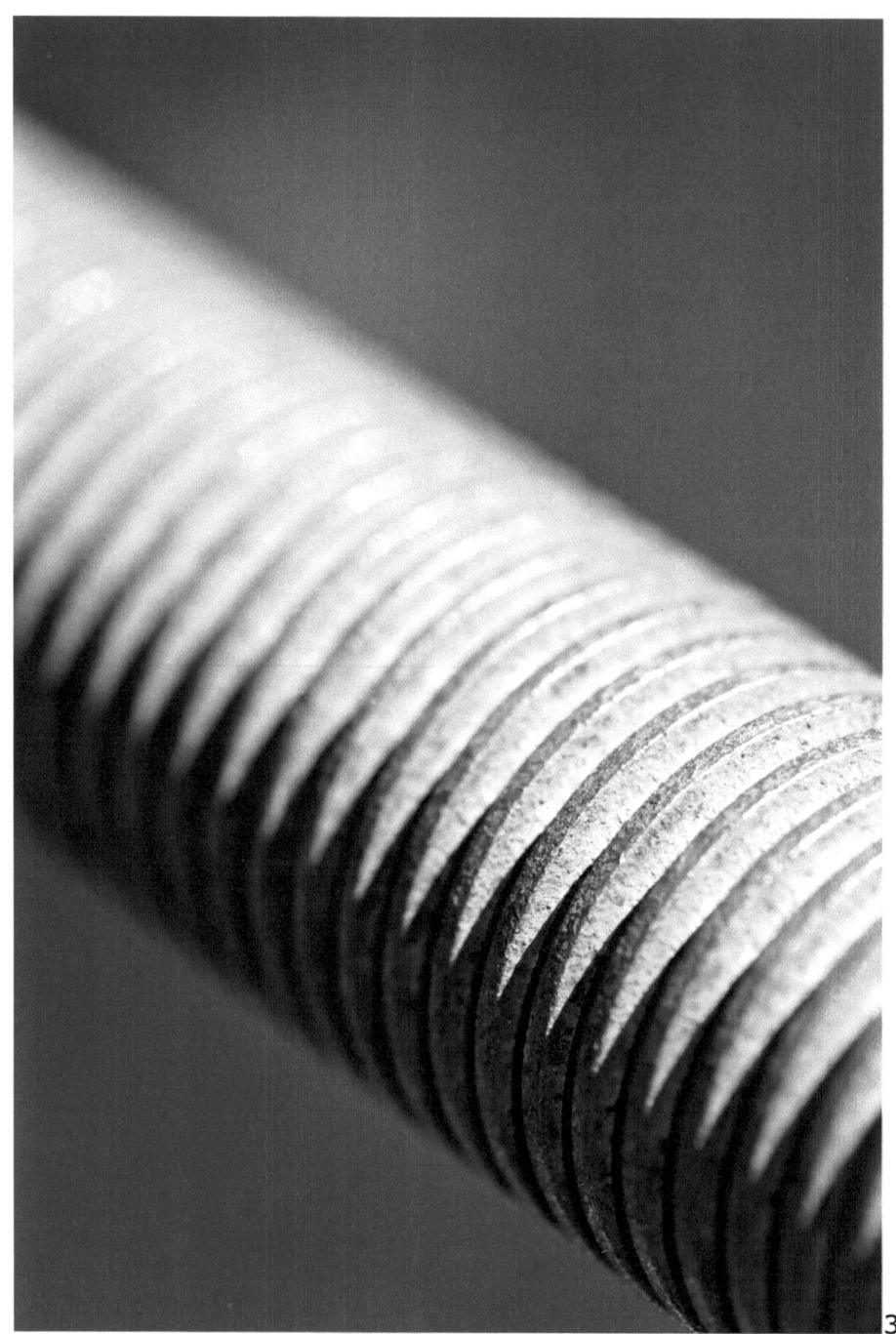

3937

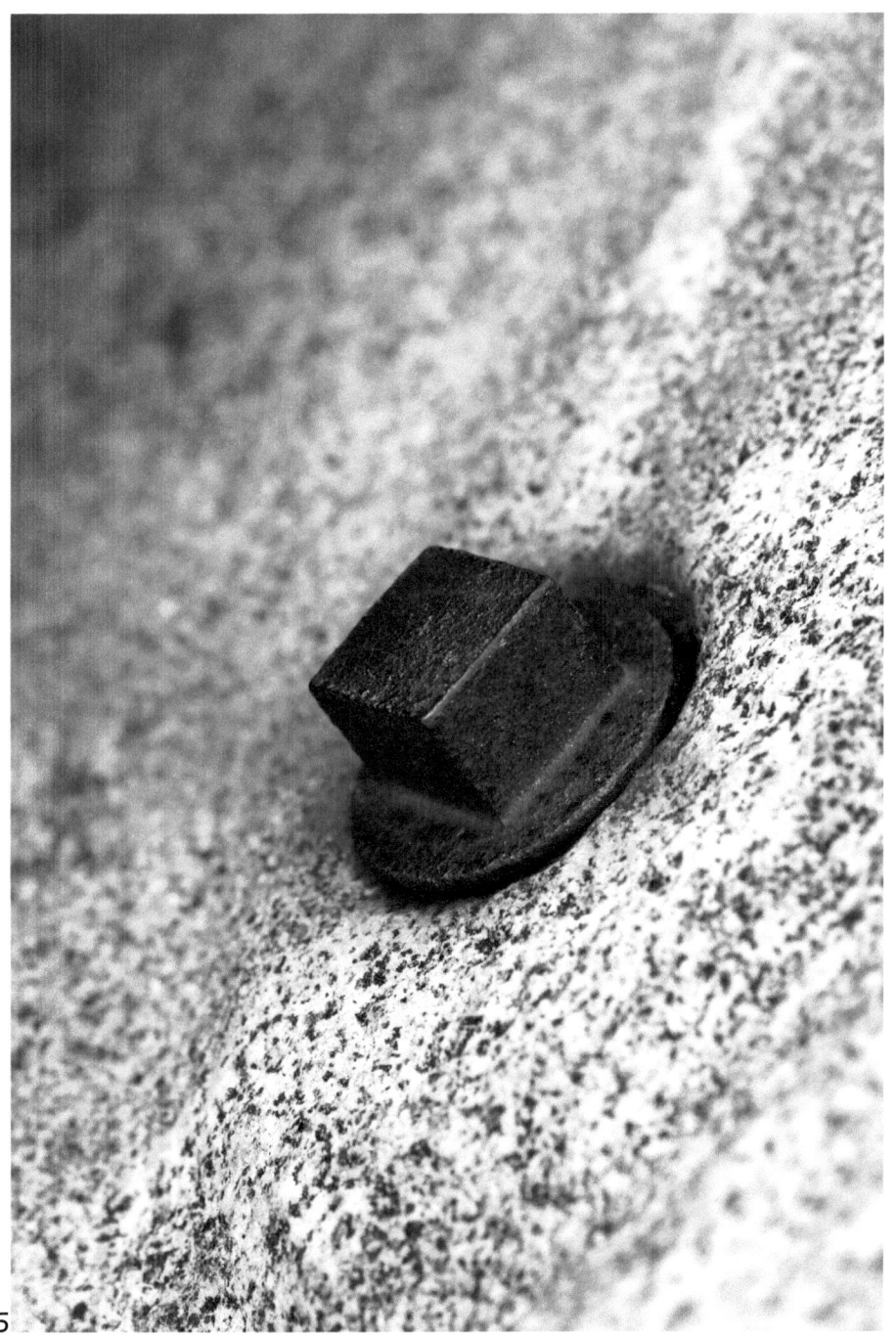

4035

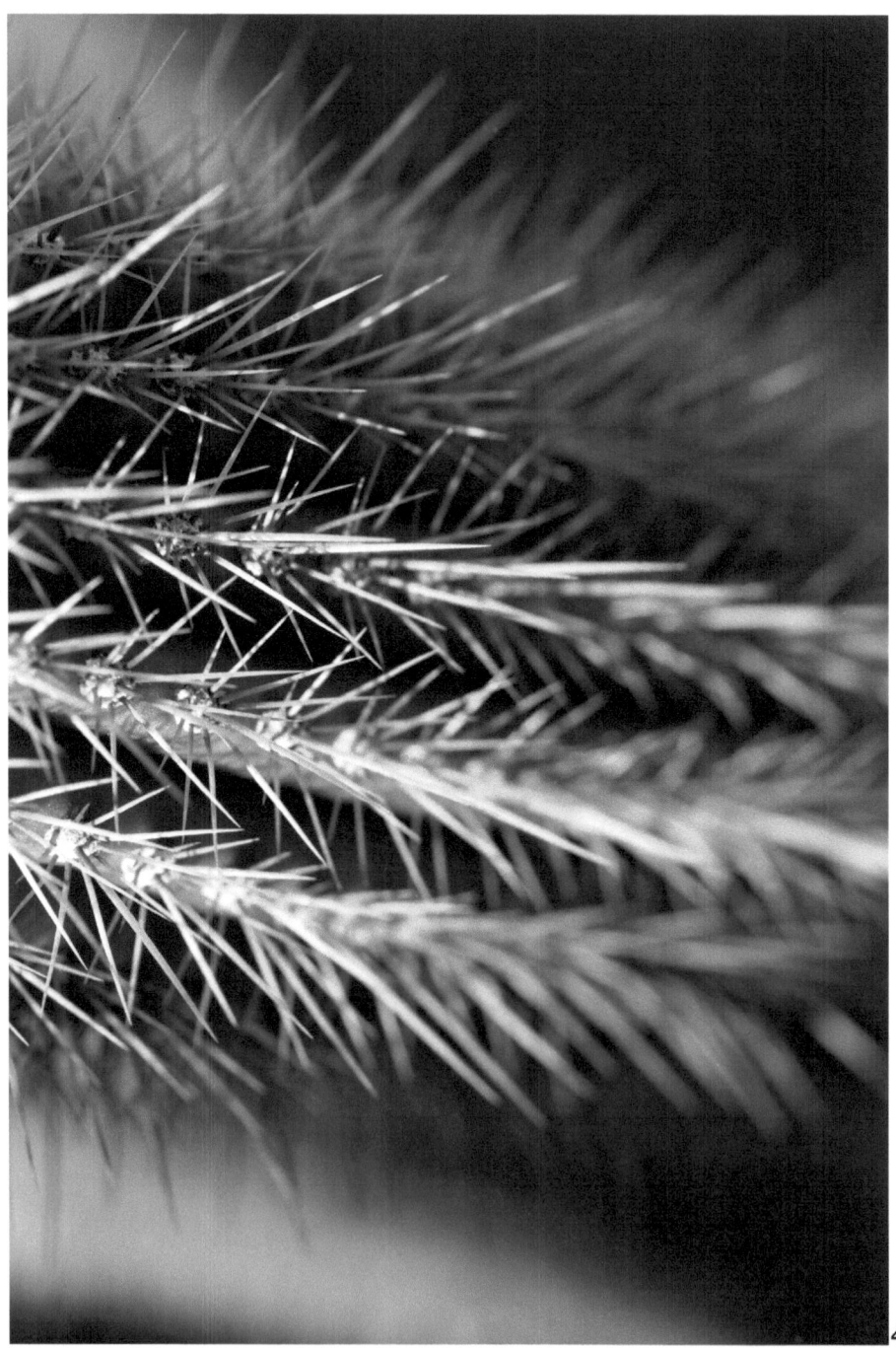

4070

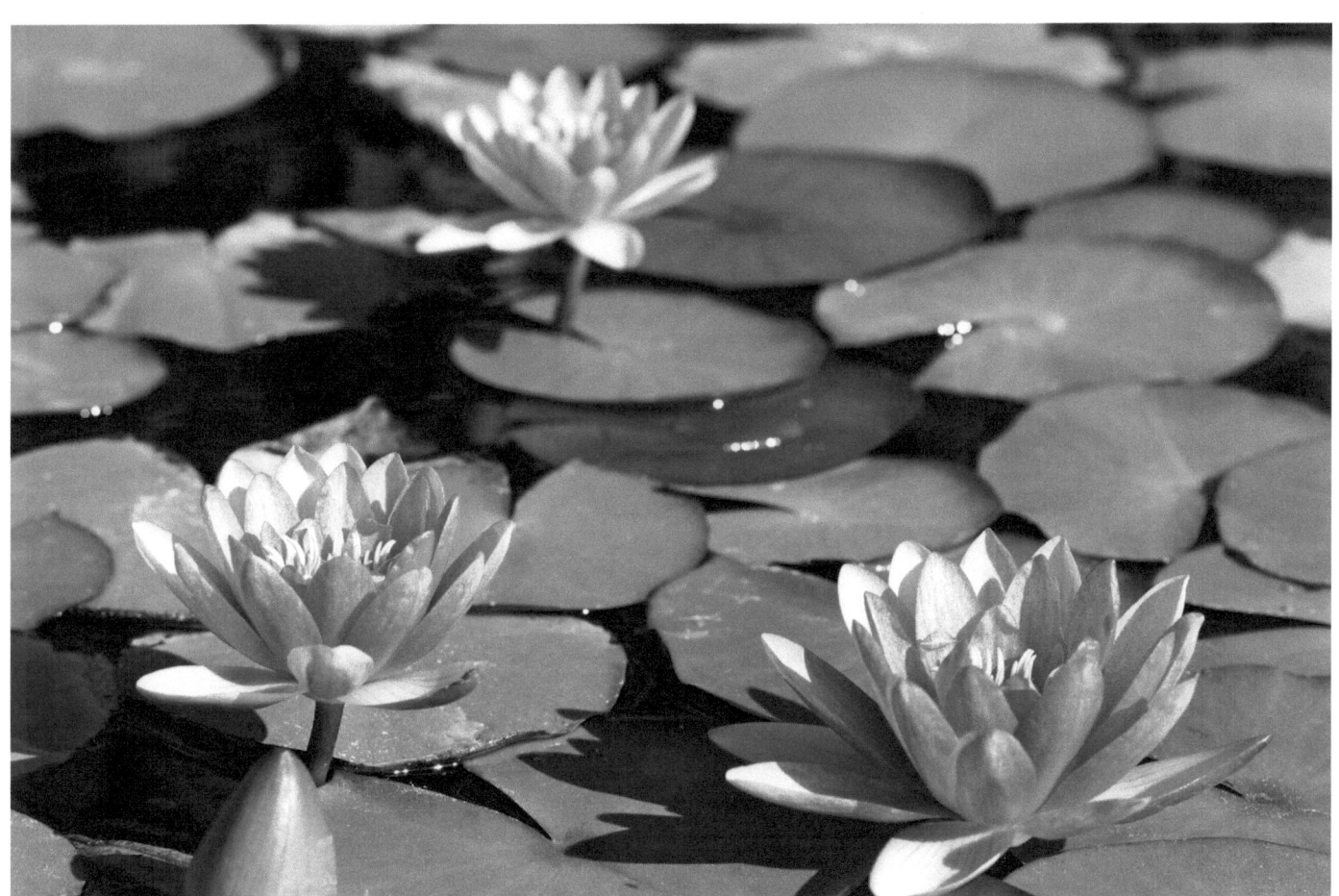

4098

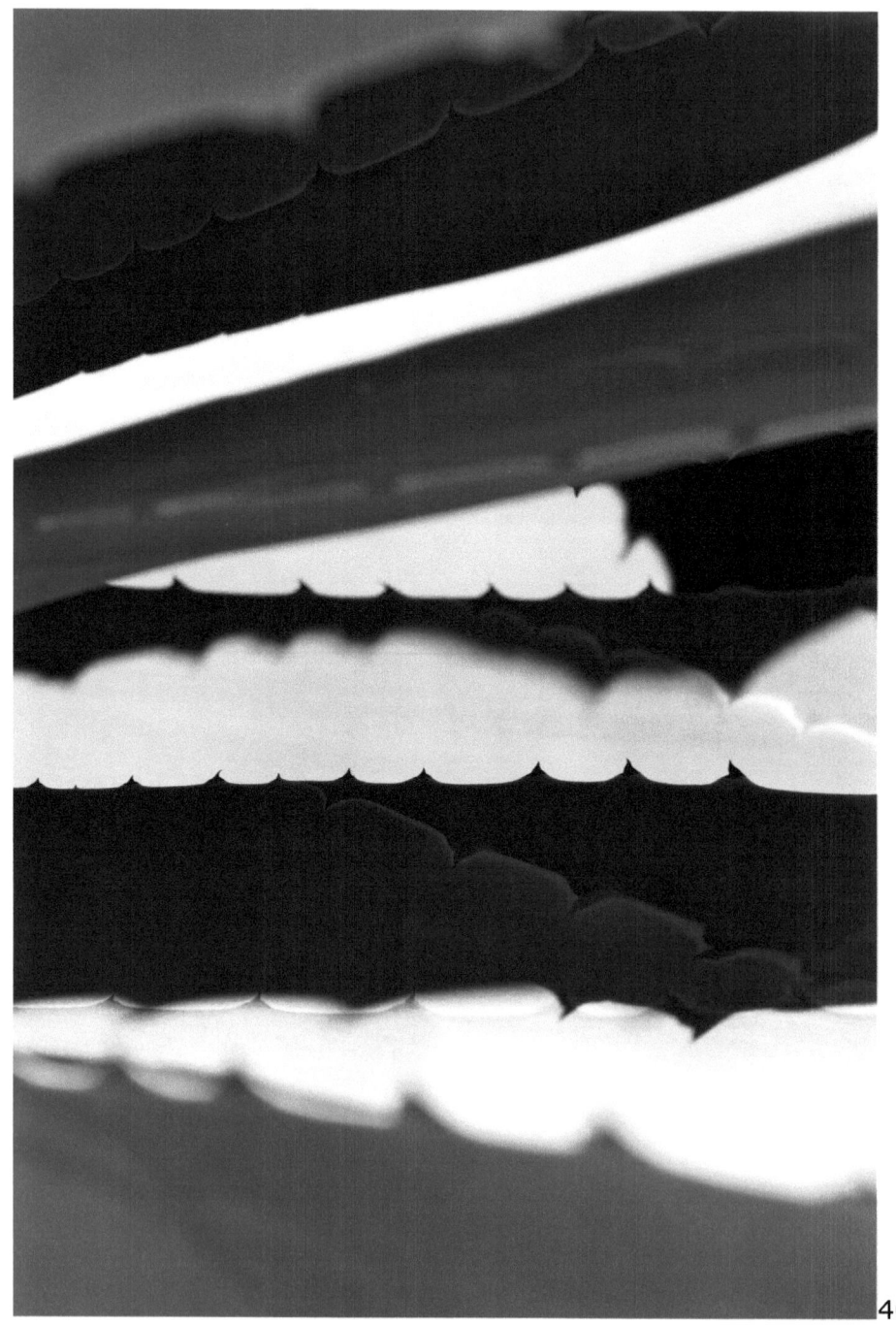

4099

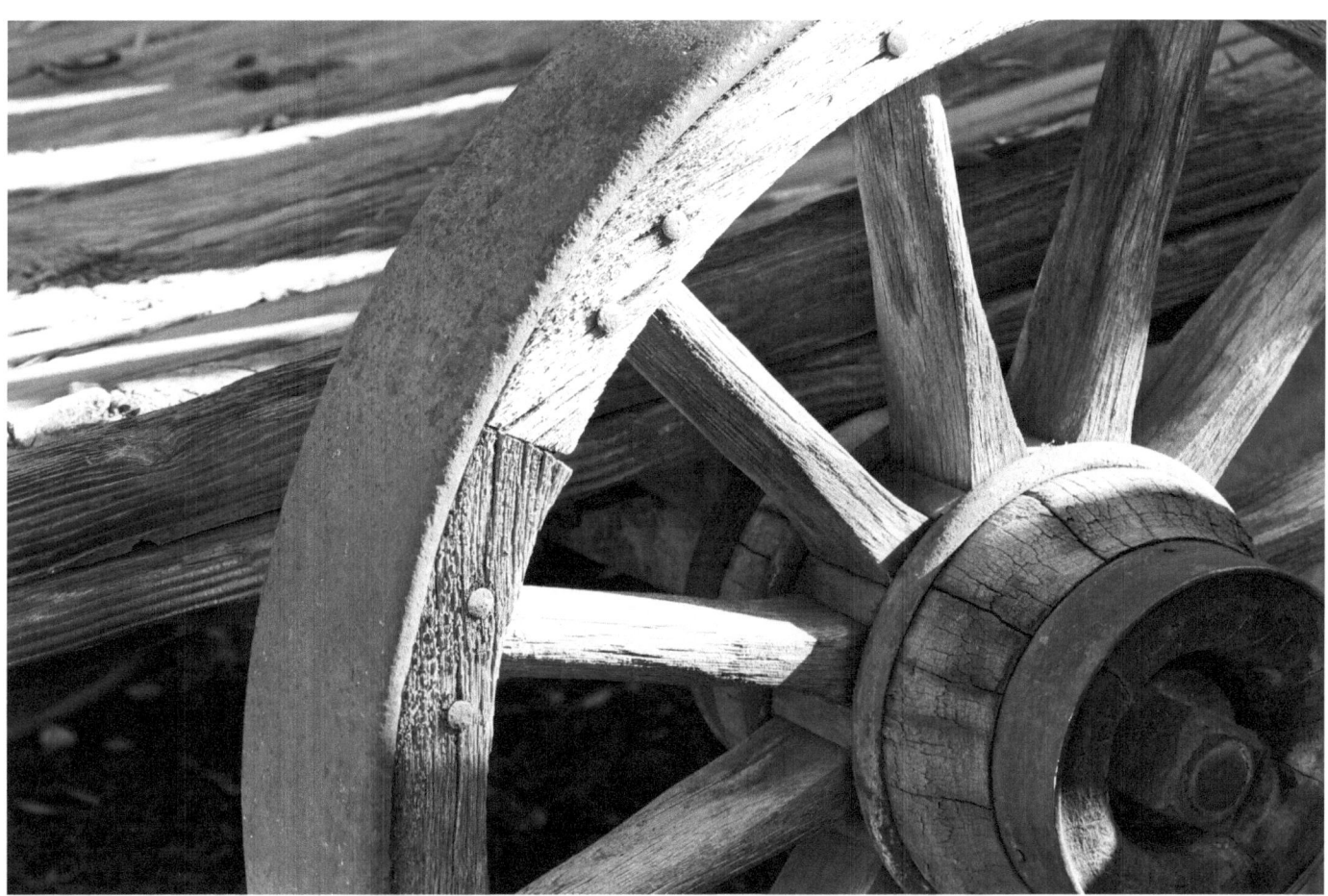

4128

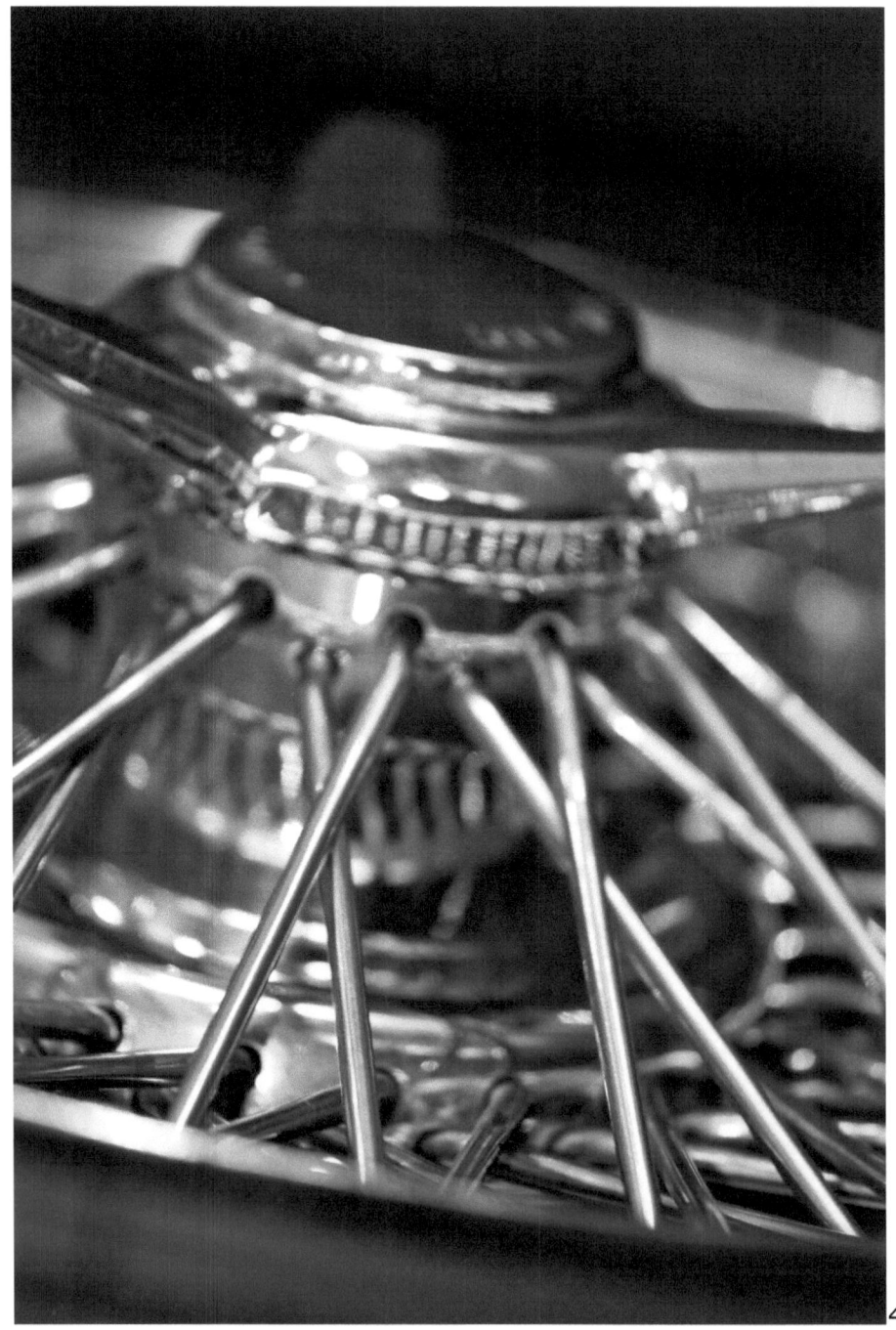

4193

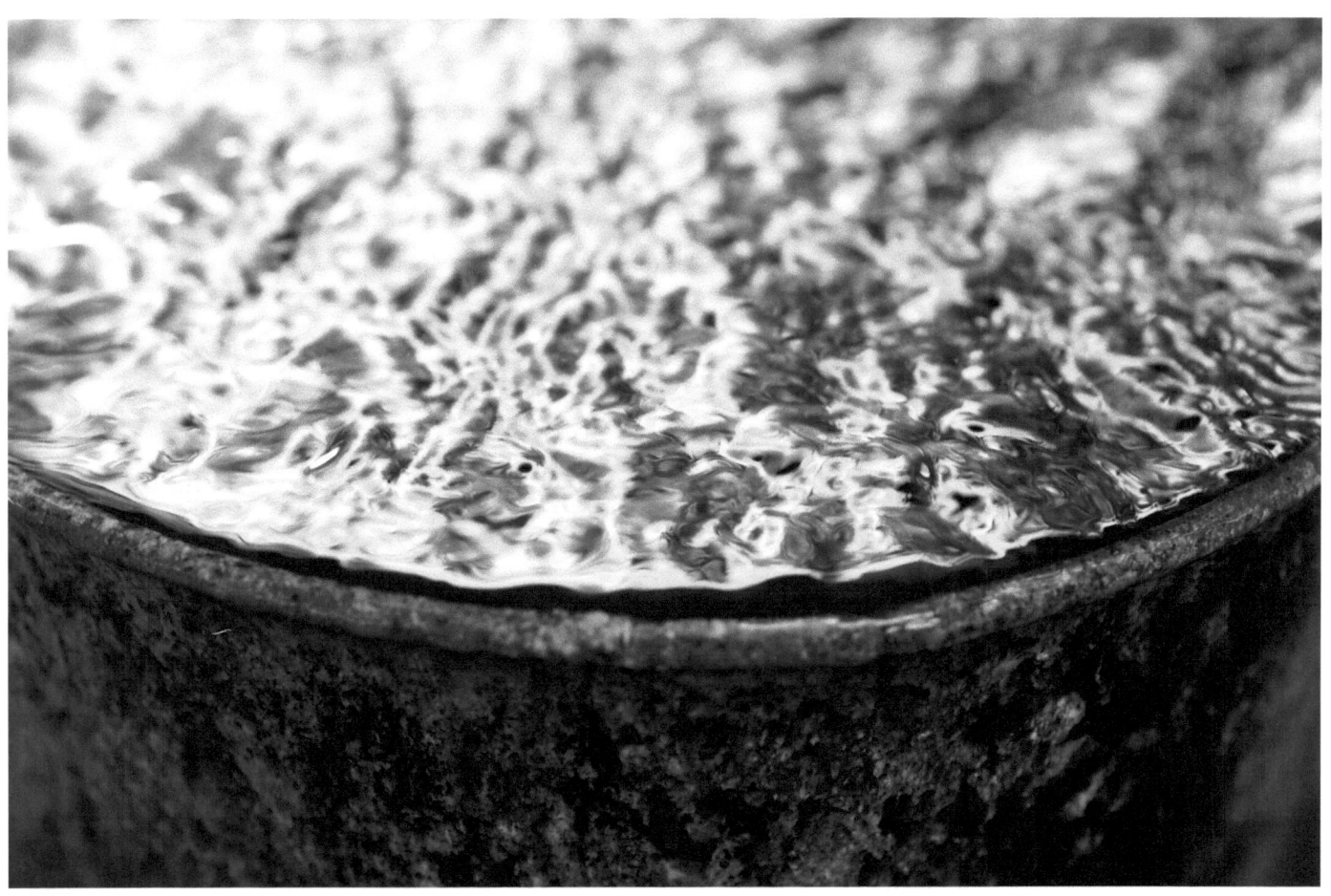

4533

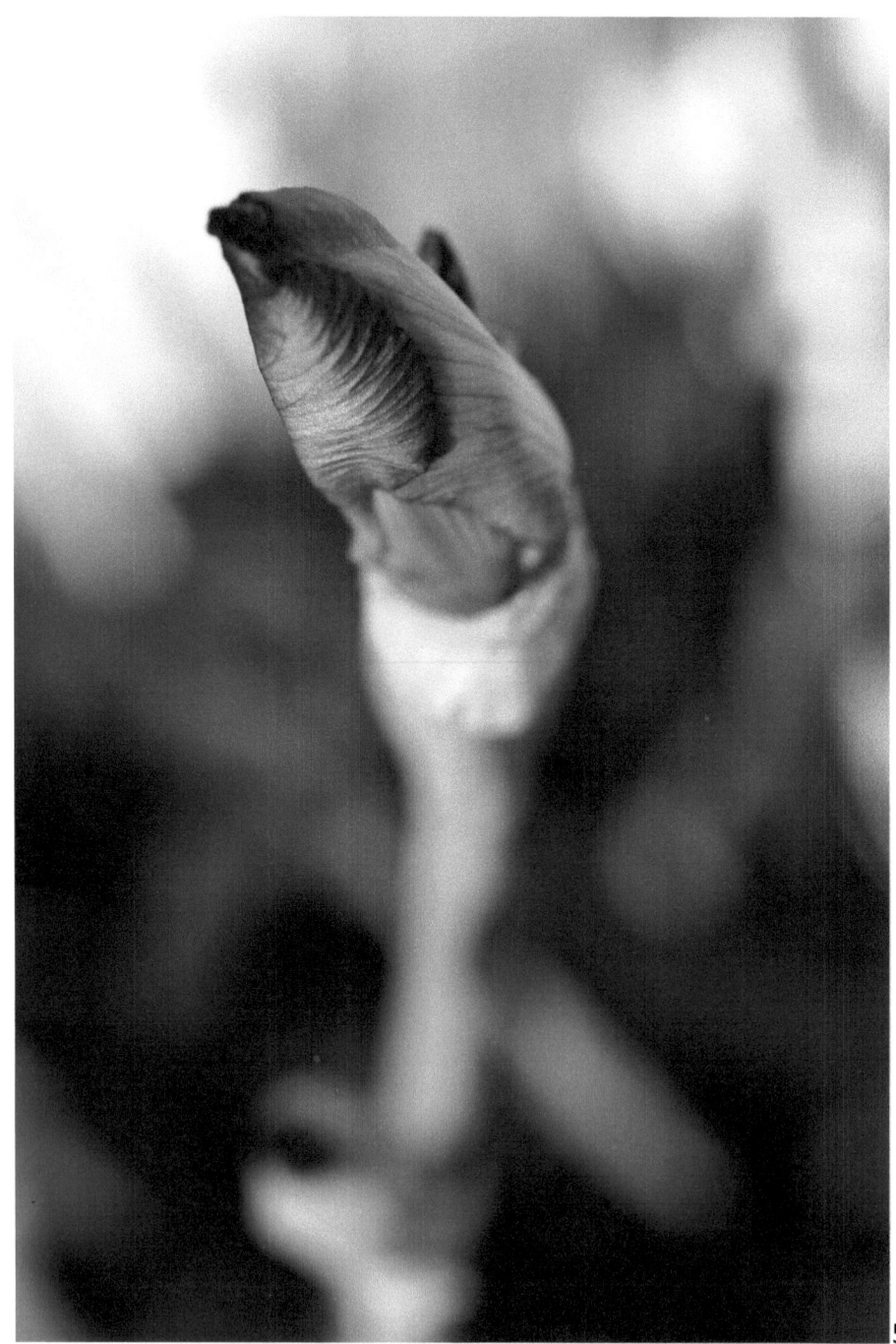

5492

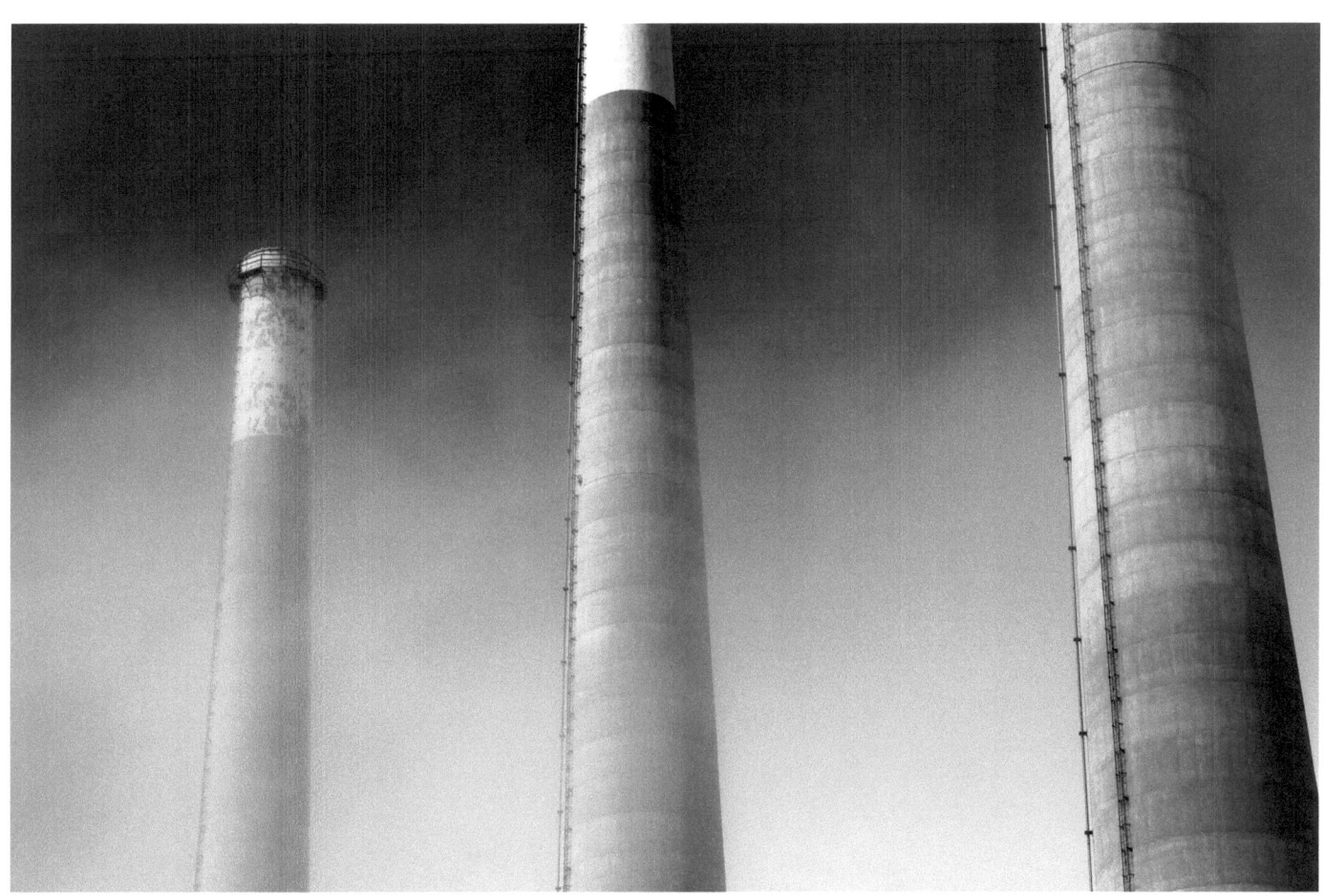

5541

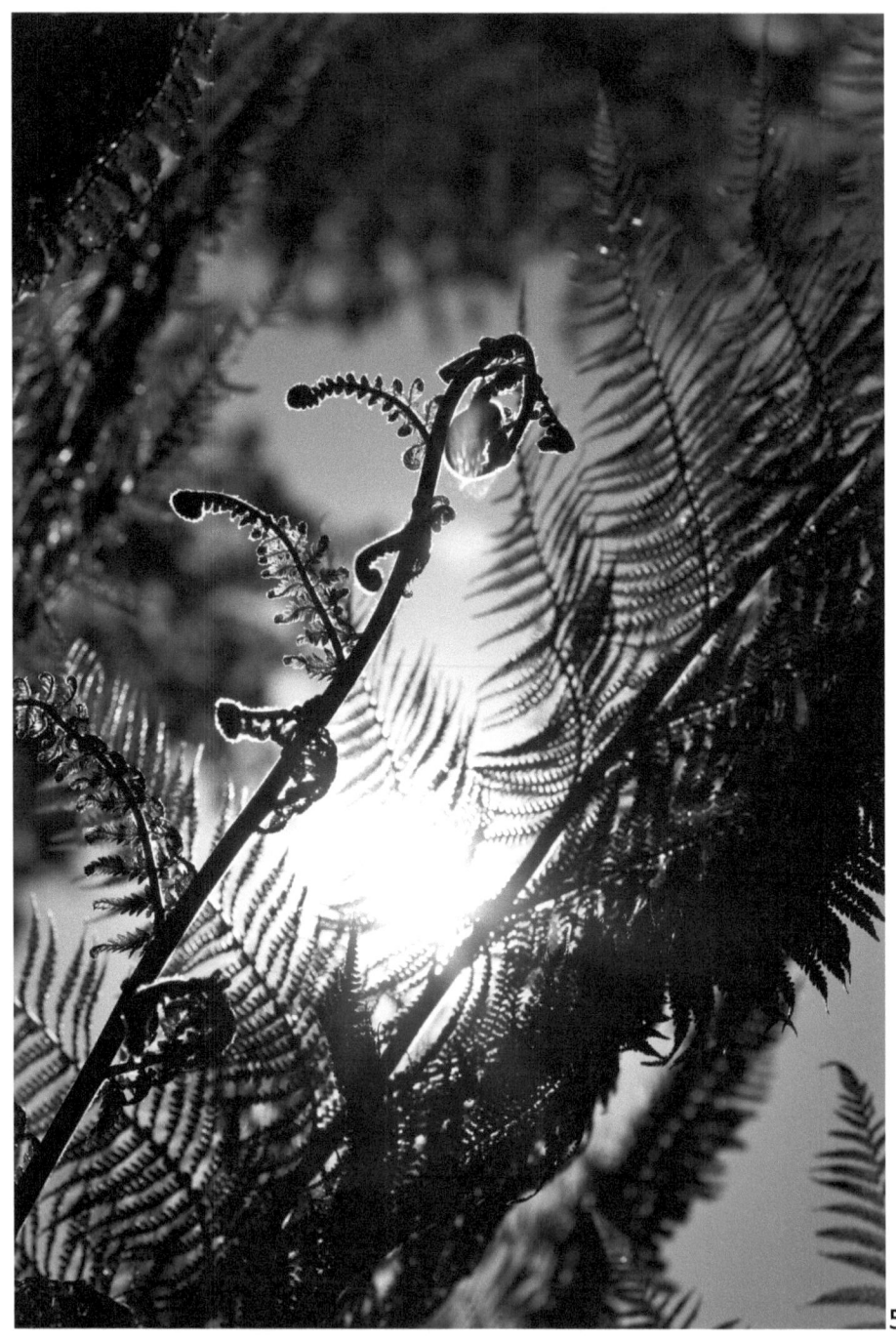

5705

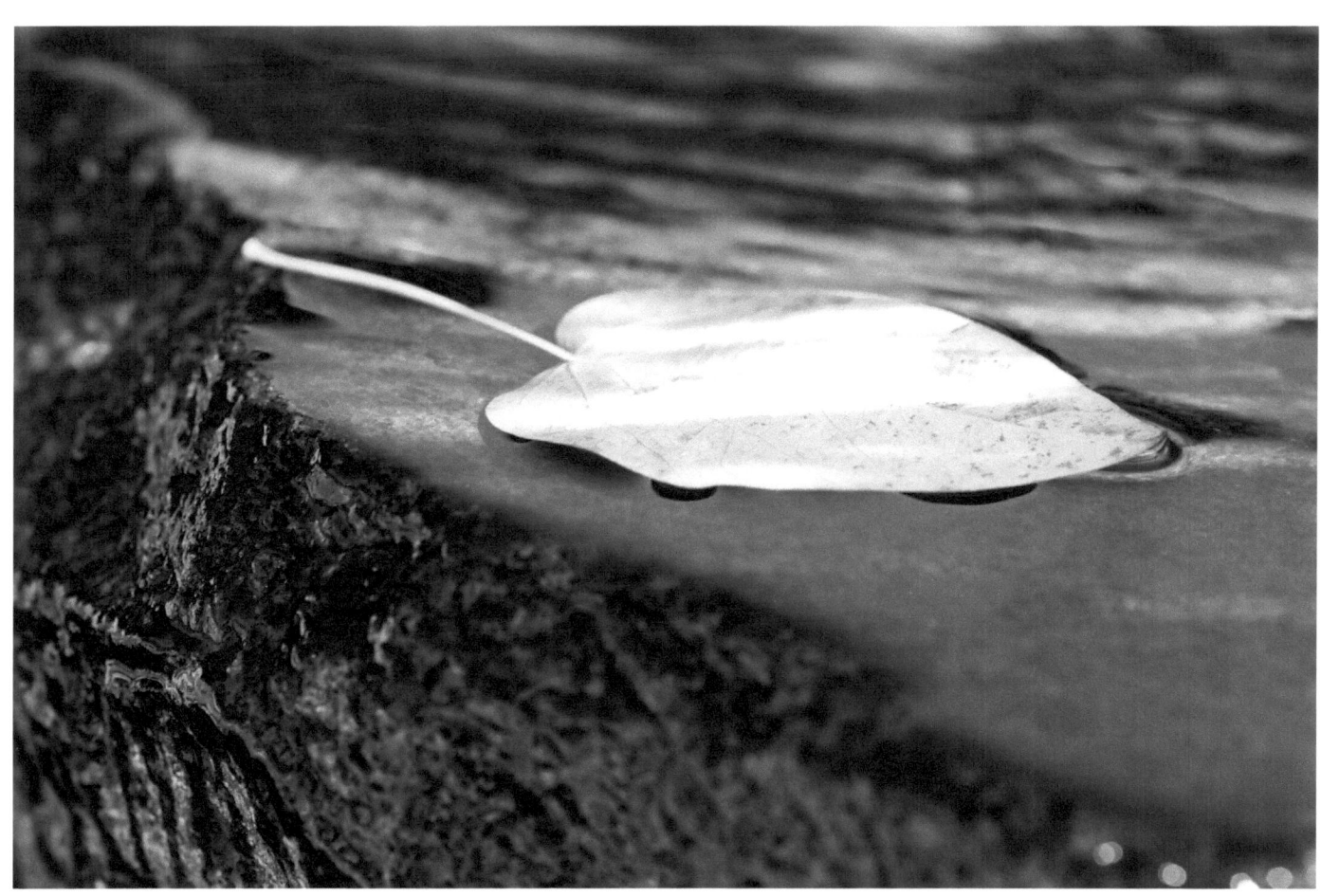

5750

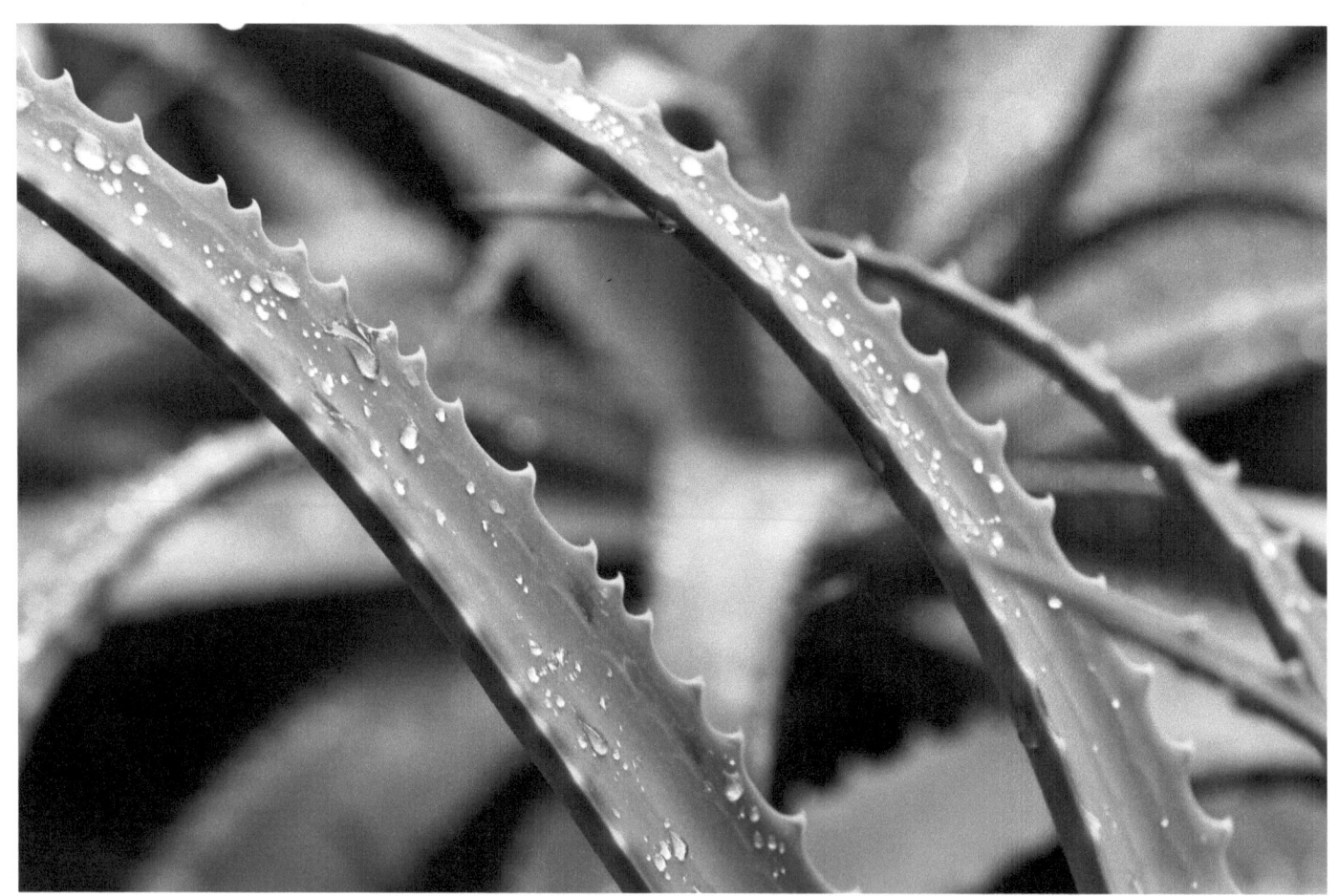

5784

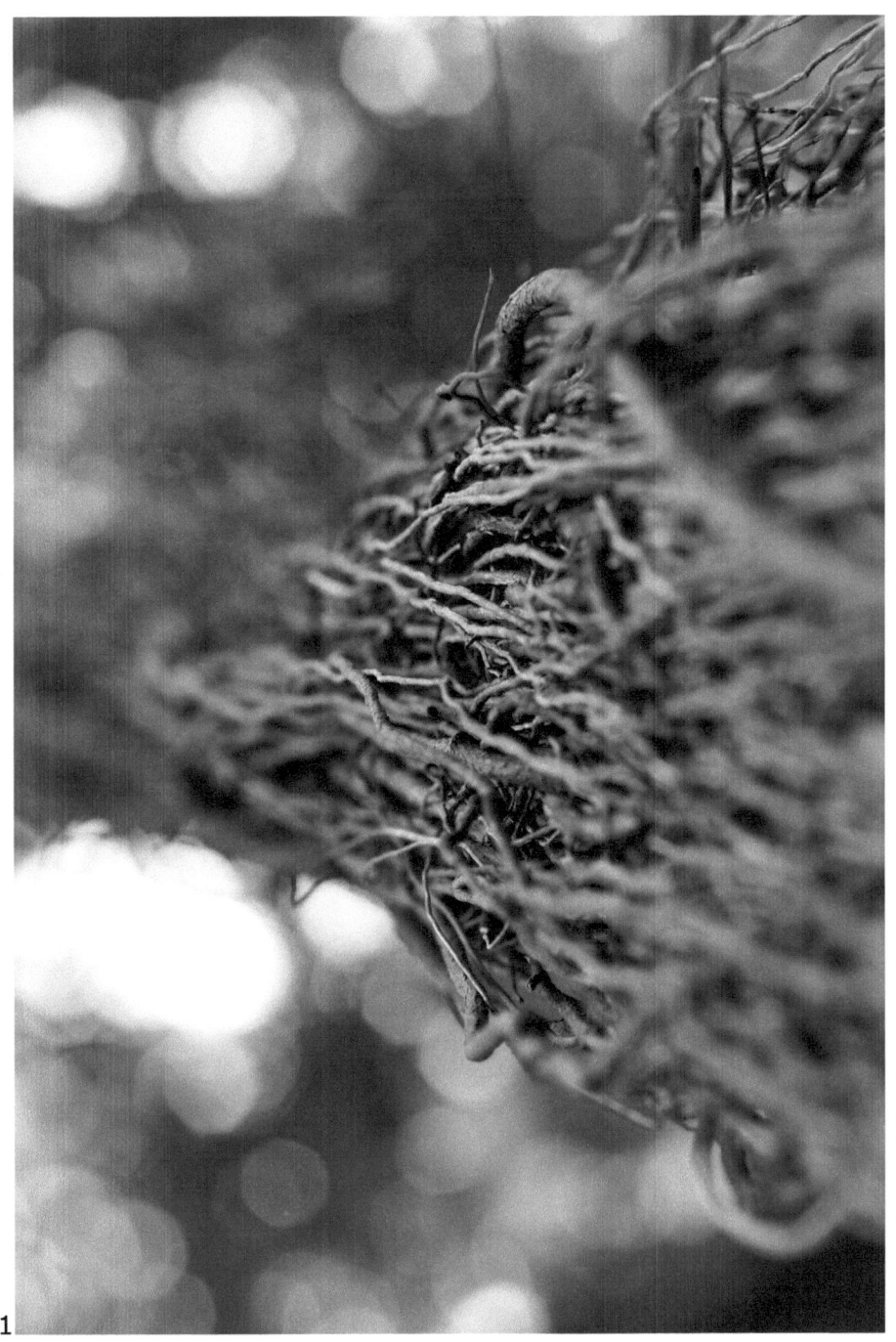

5811

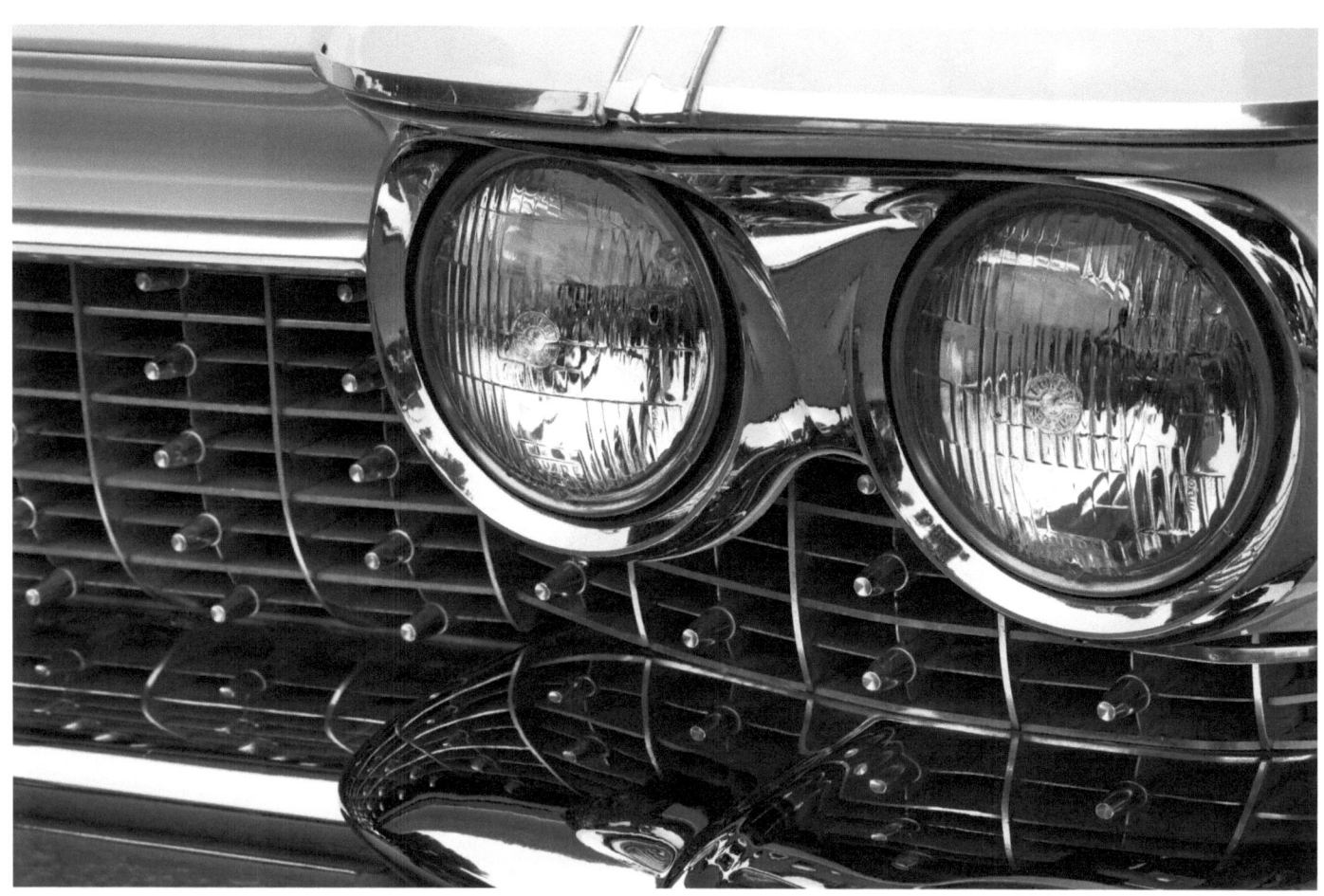

5844

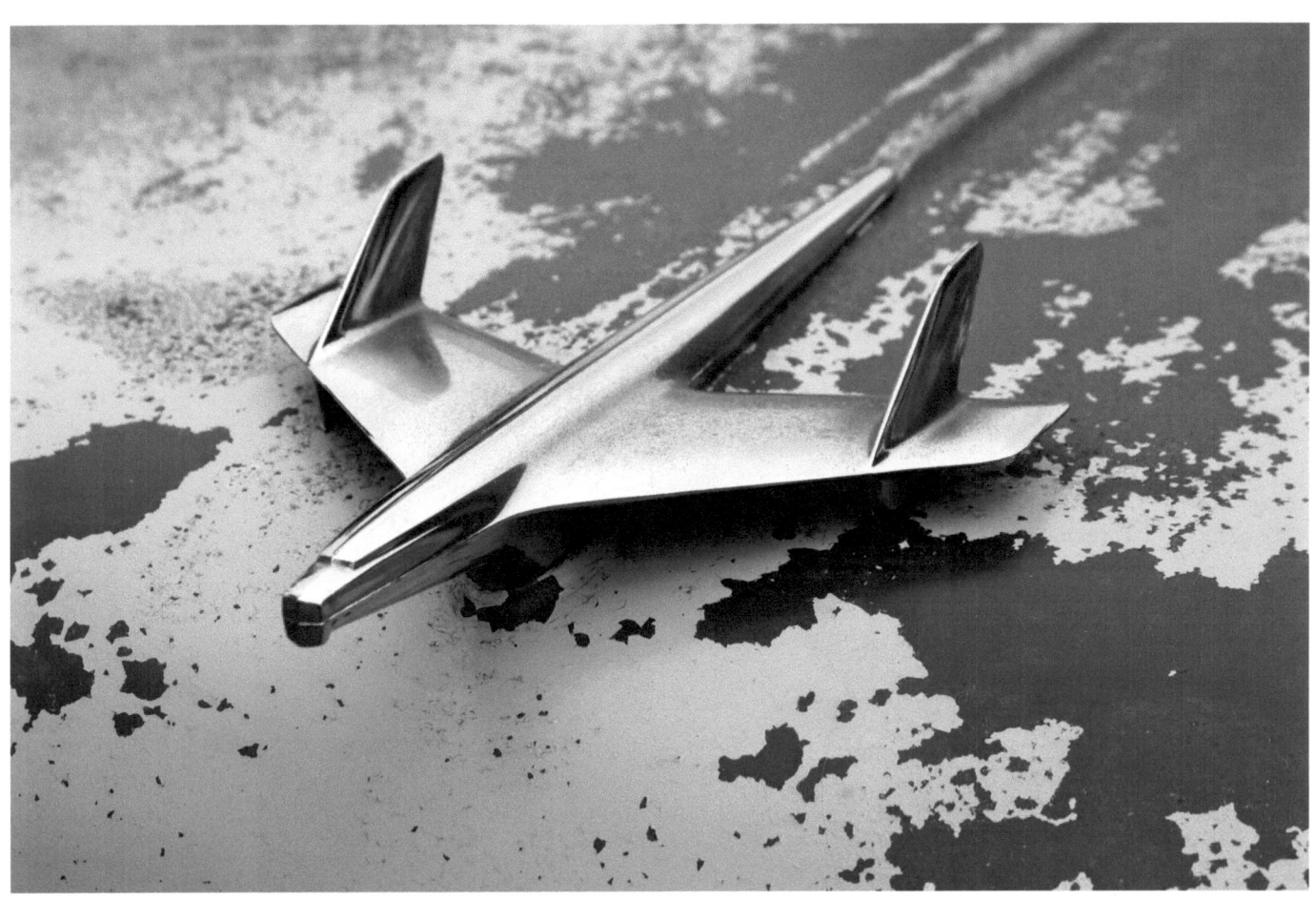

5846

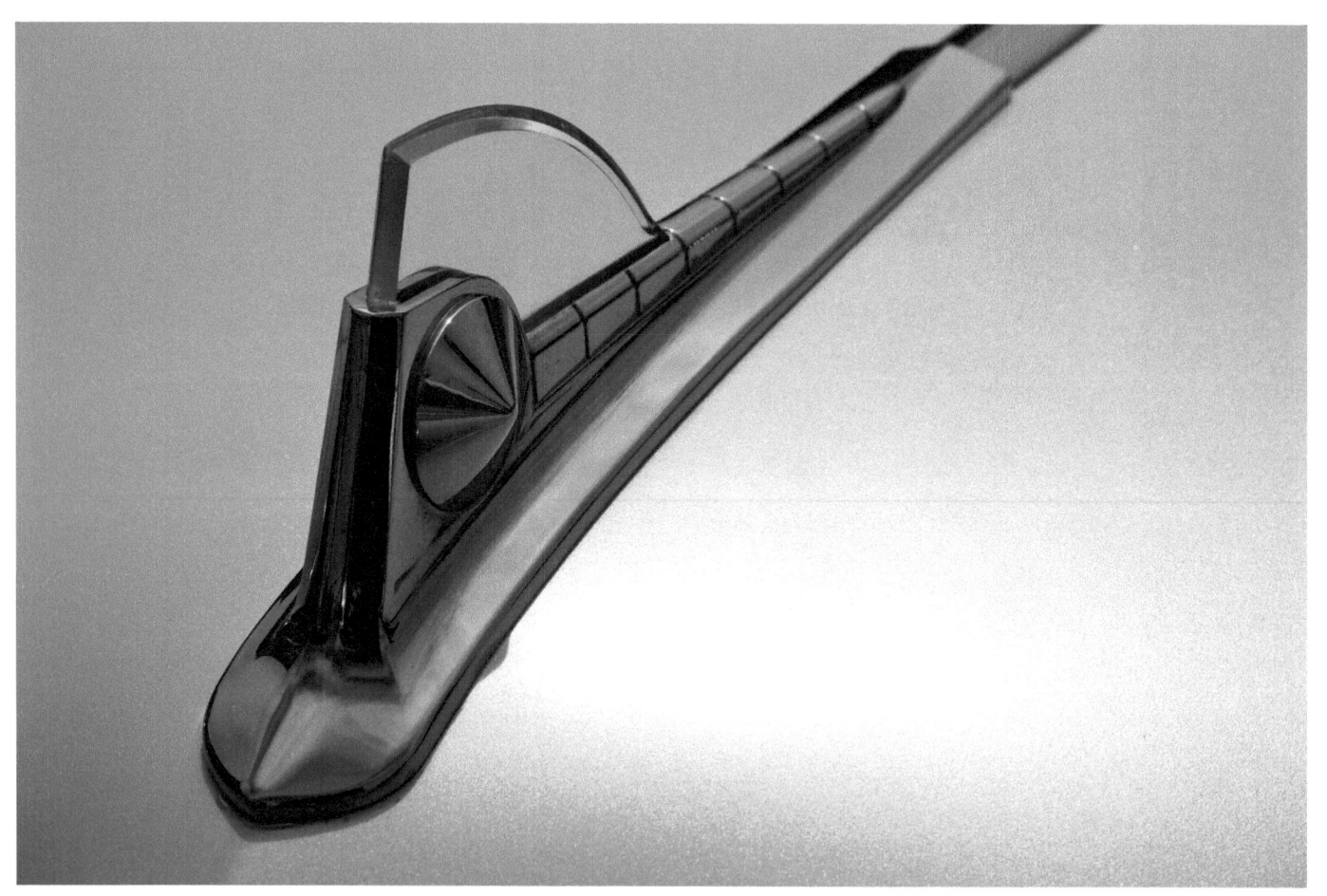

6014

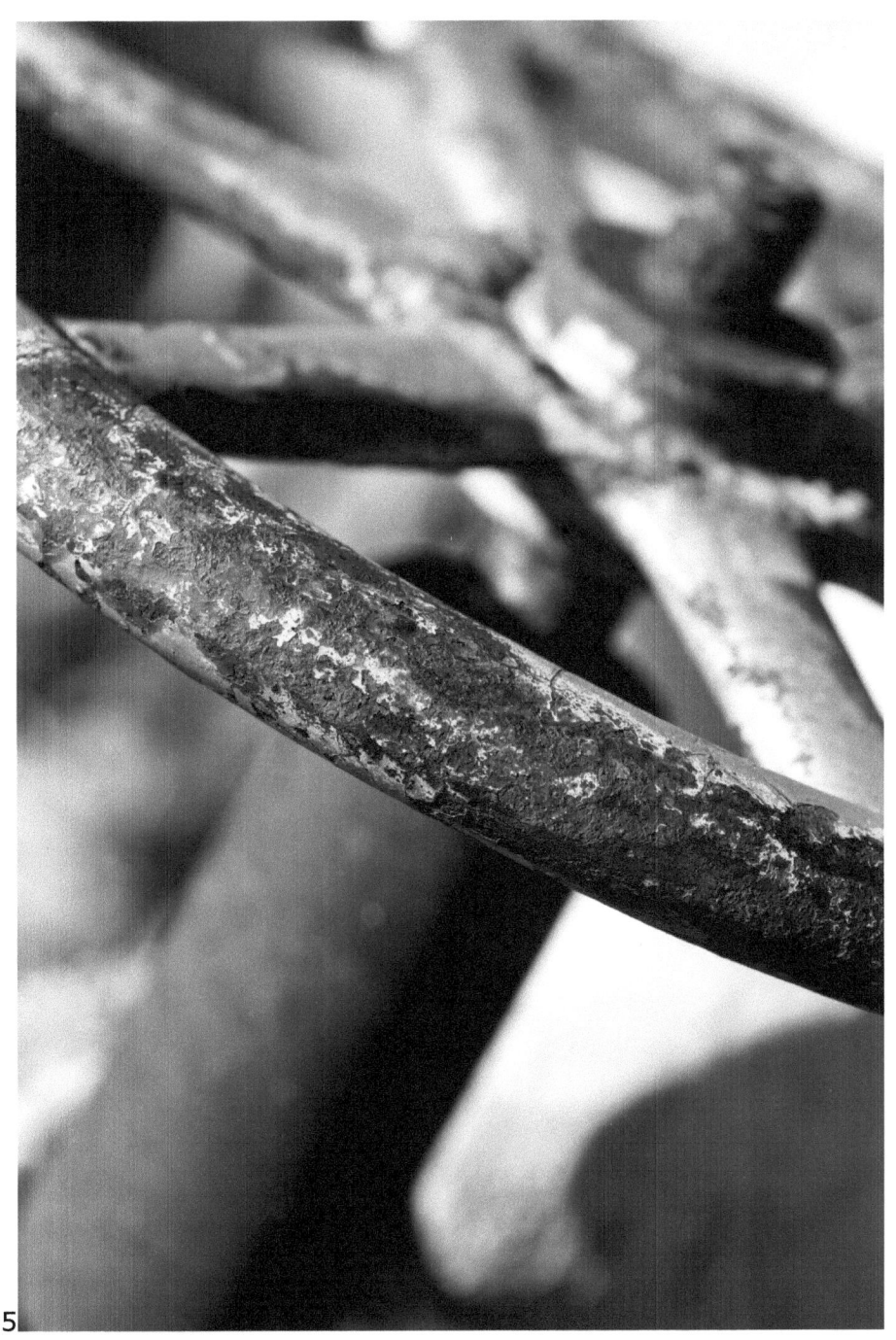

6095

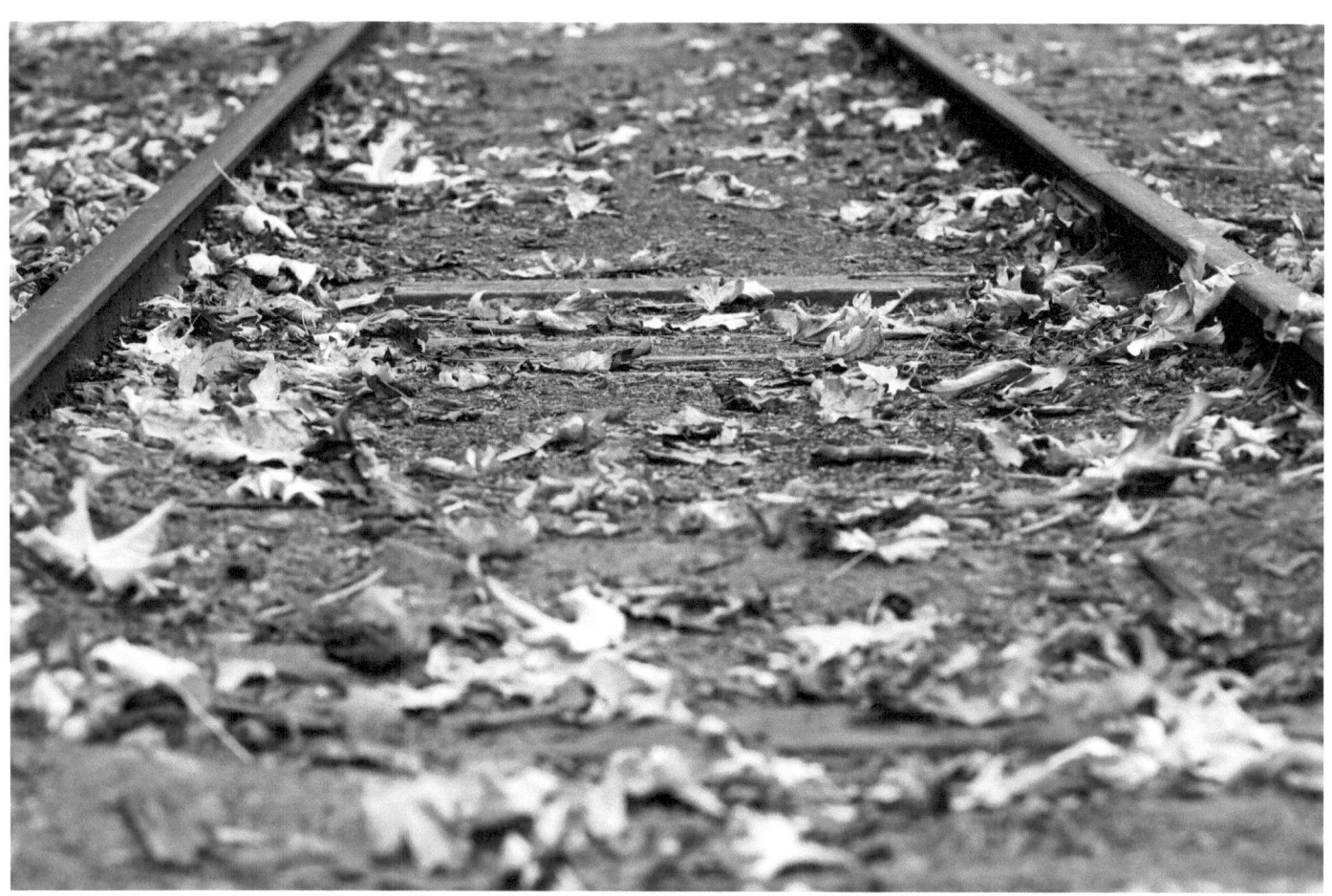

6176

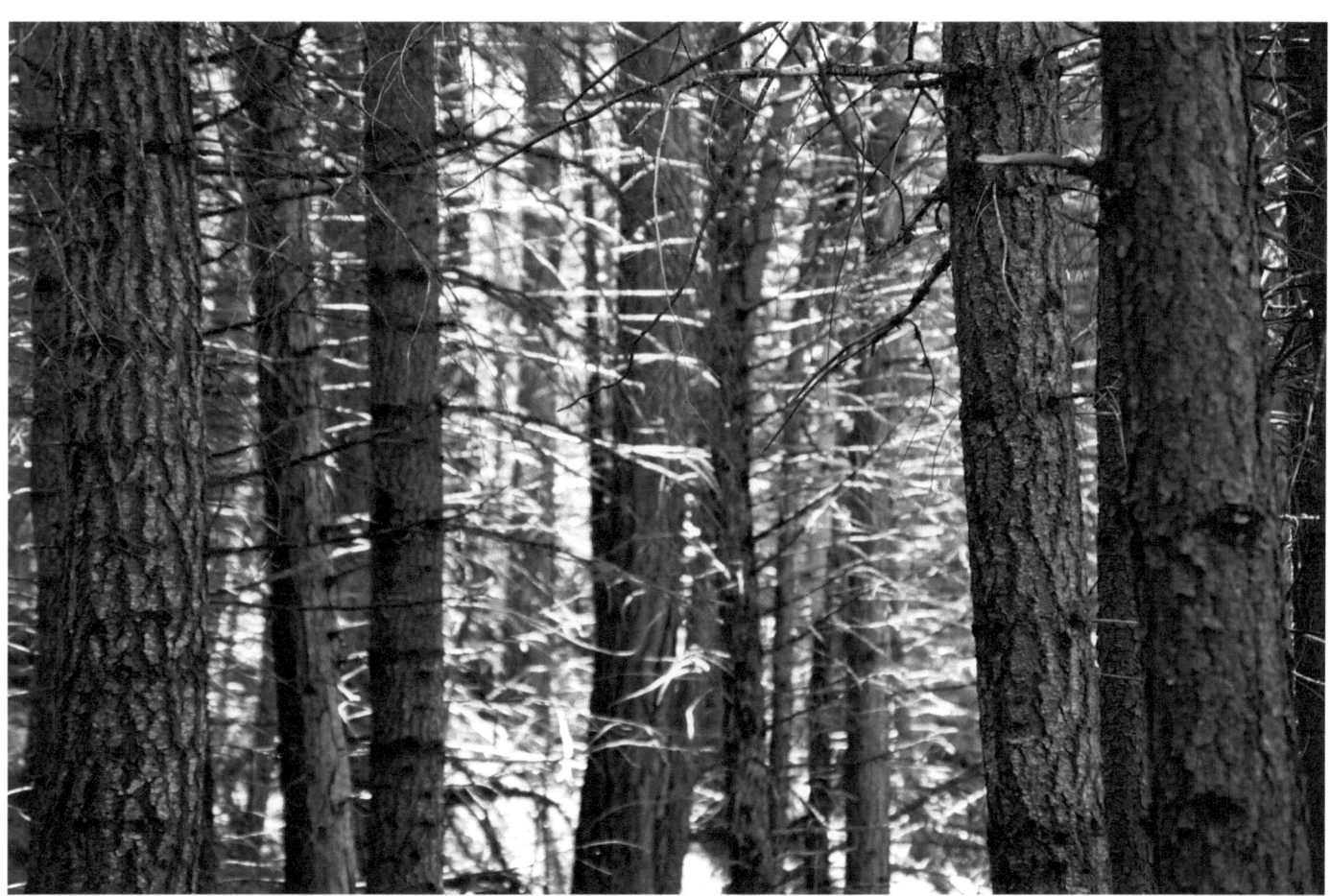

6659

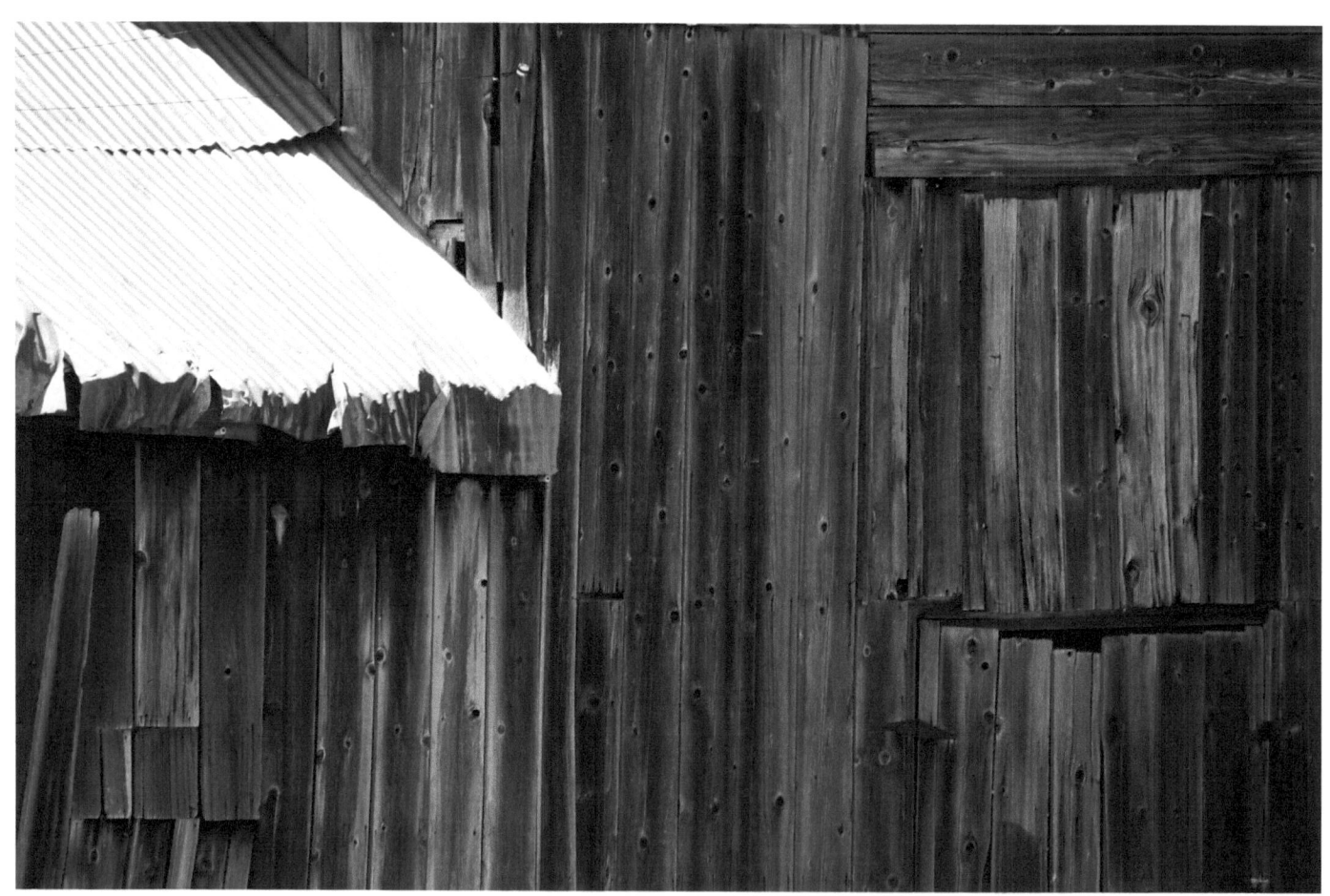

6946

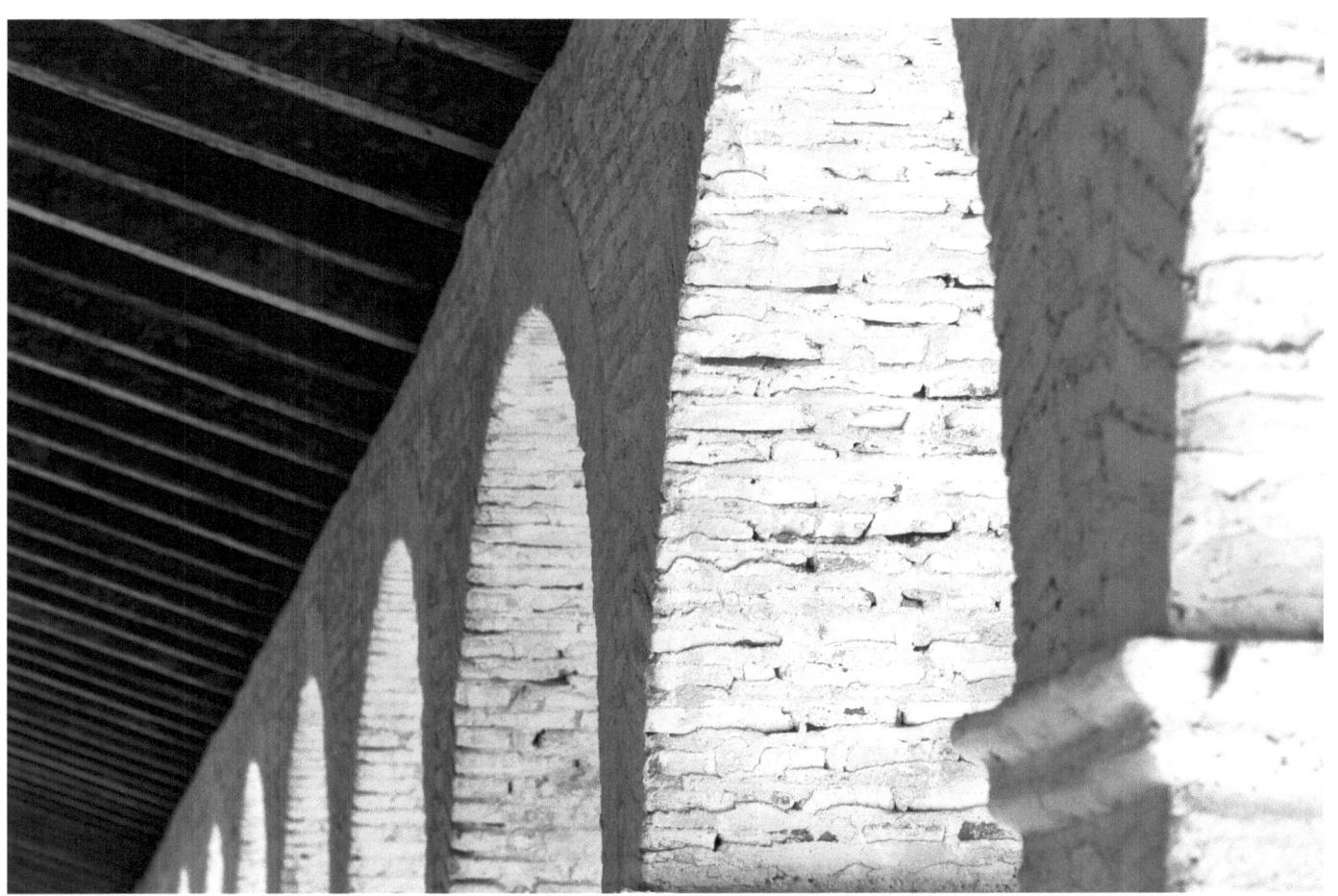

7656

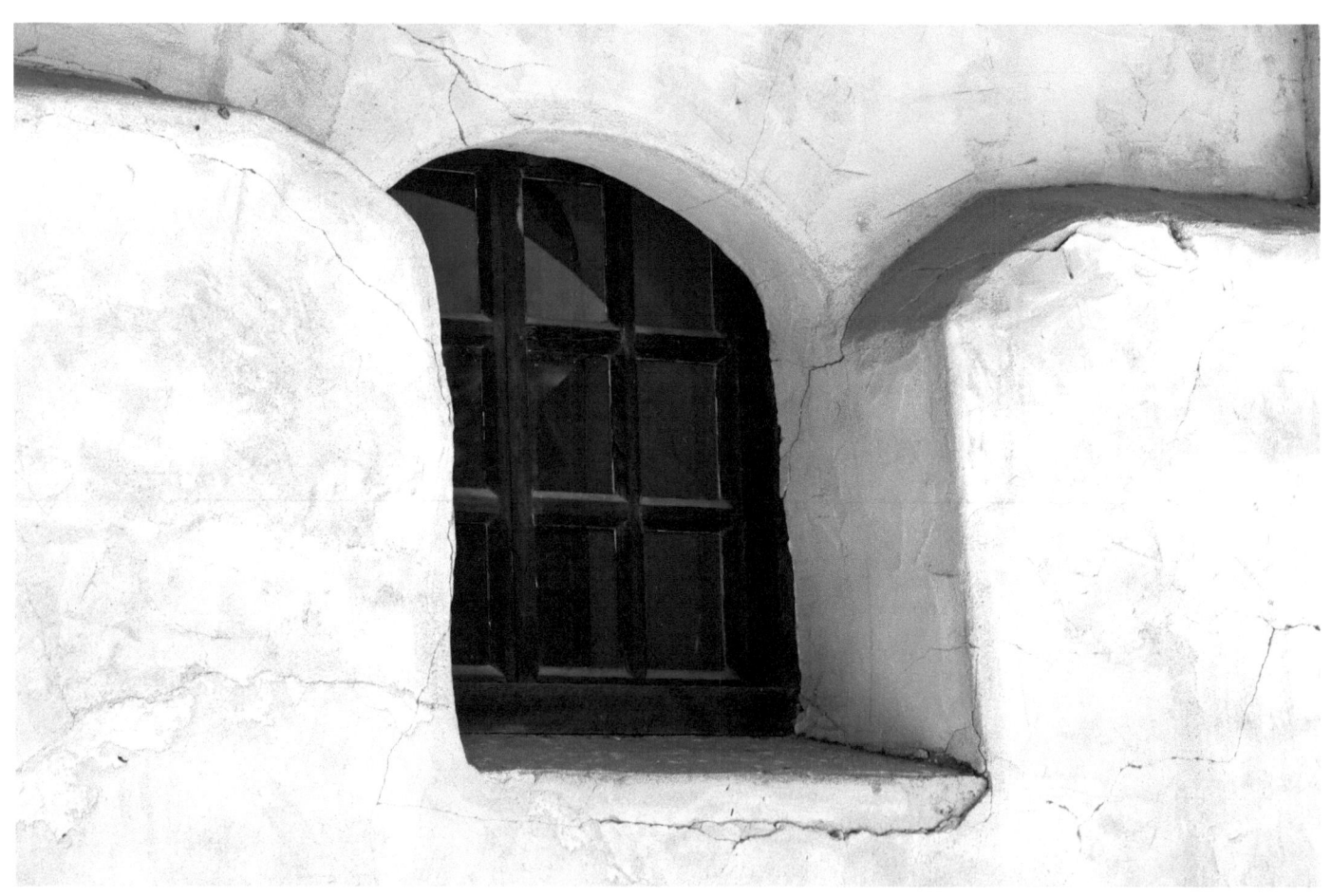

7693

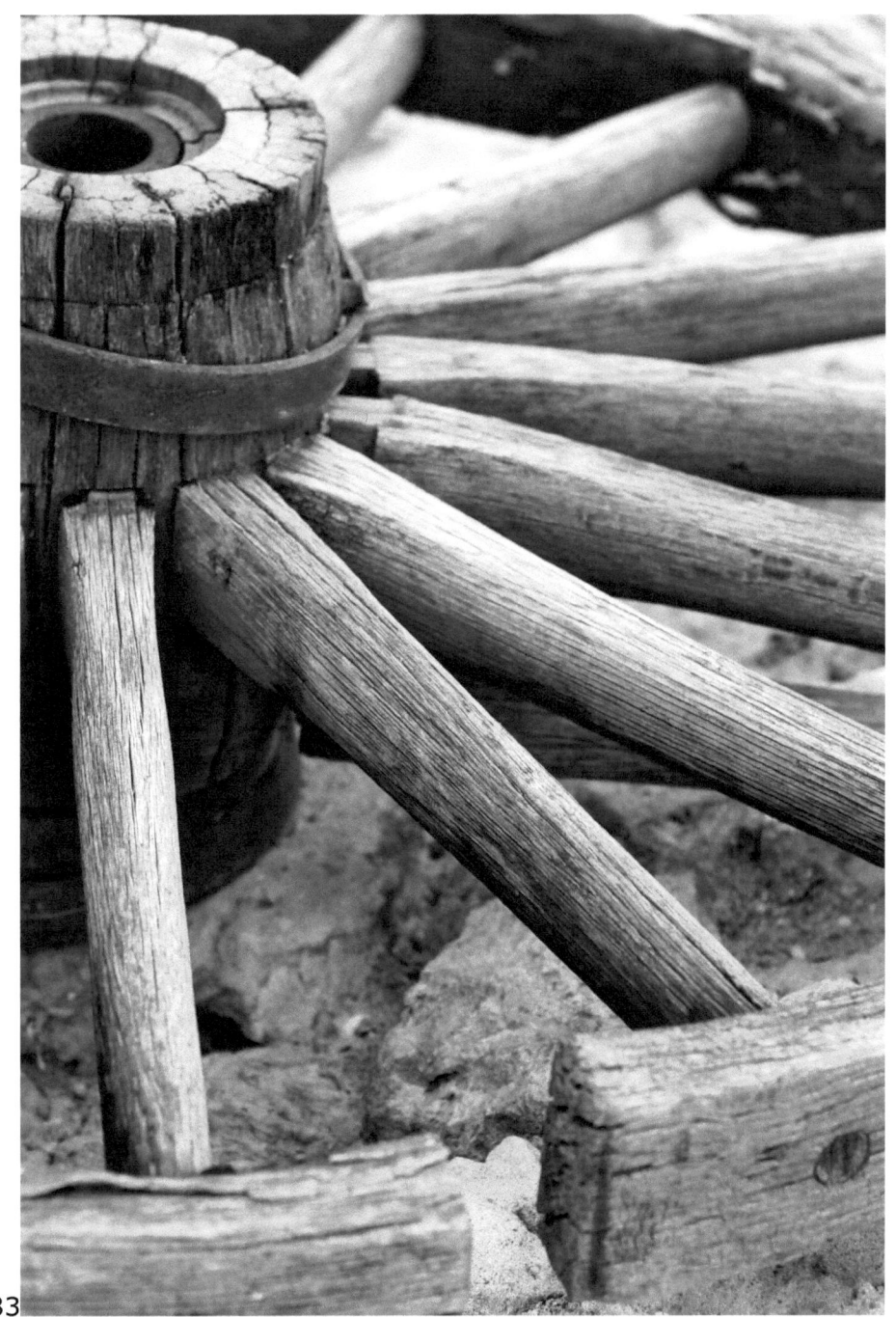

7783

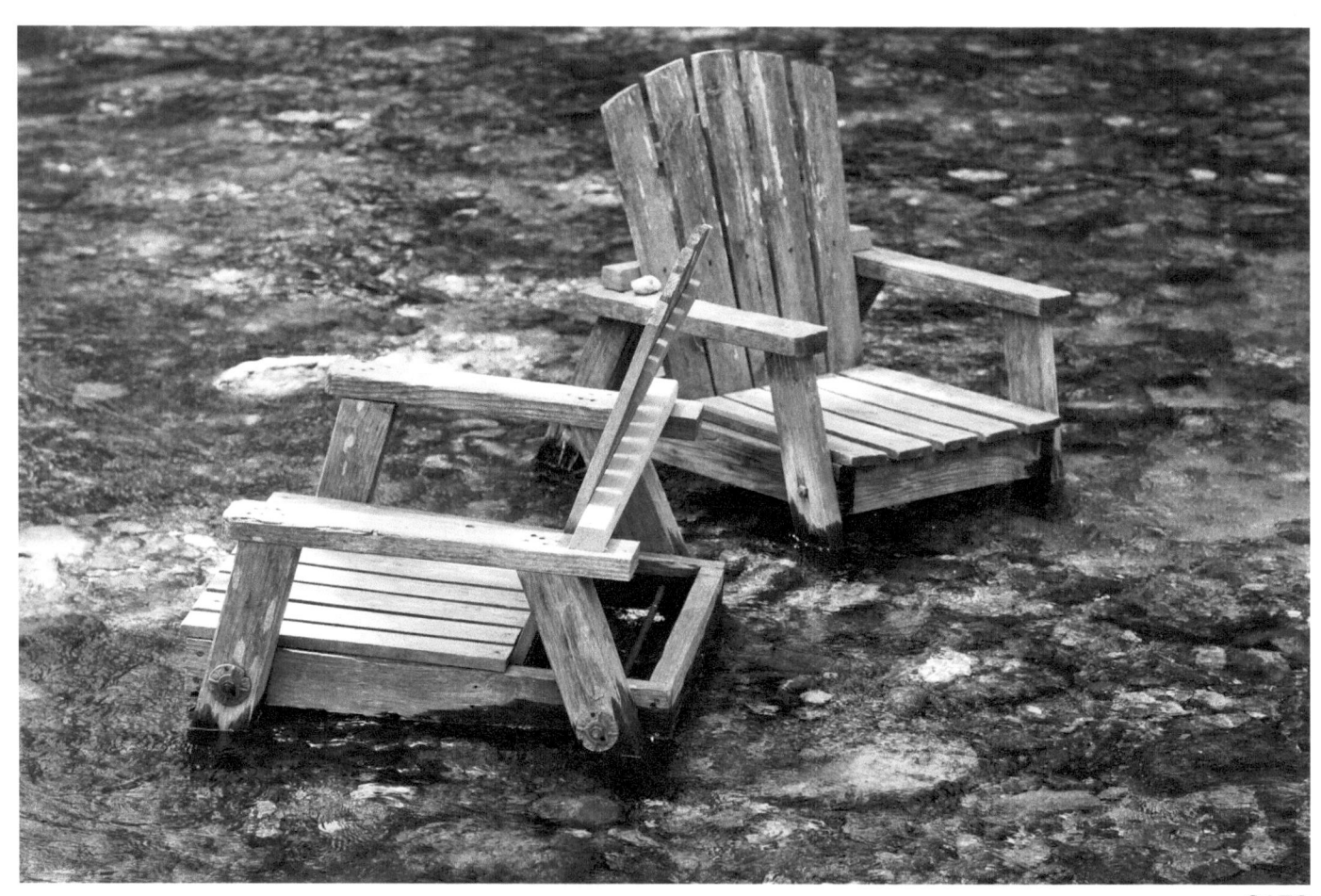

8173

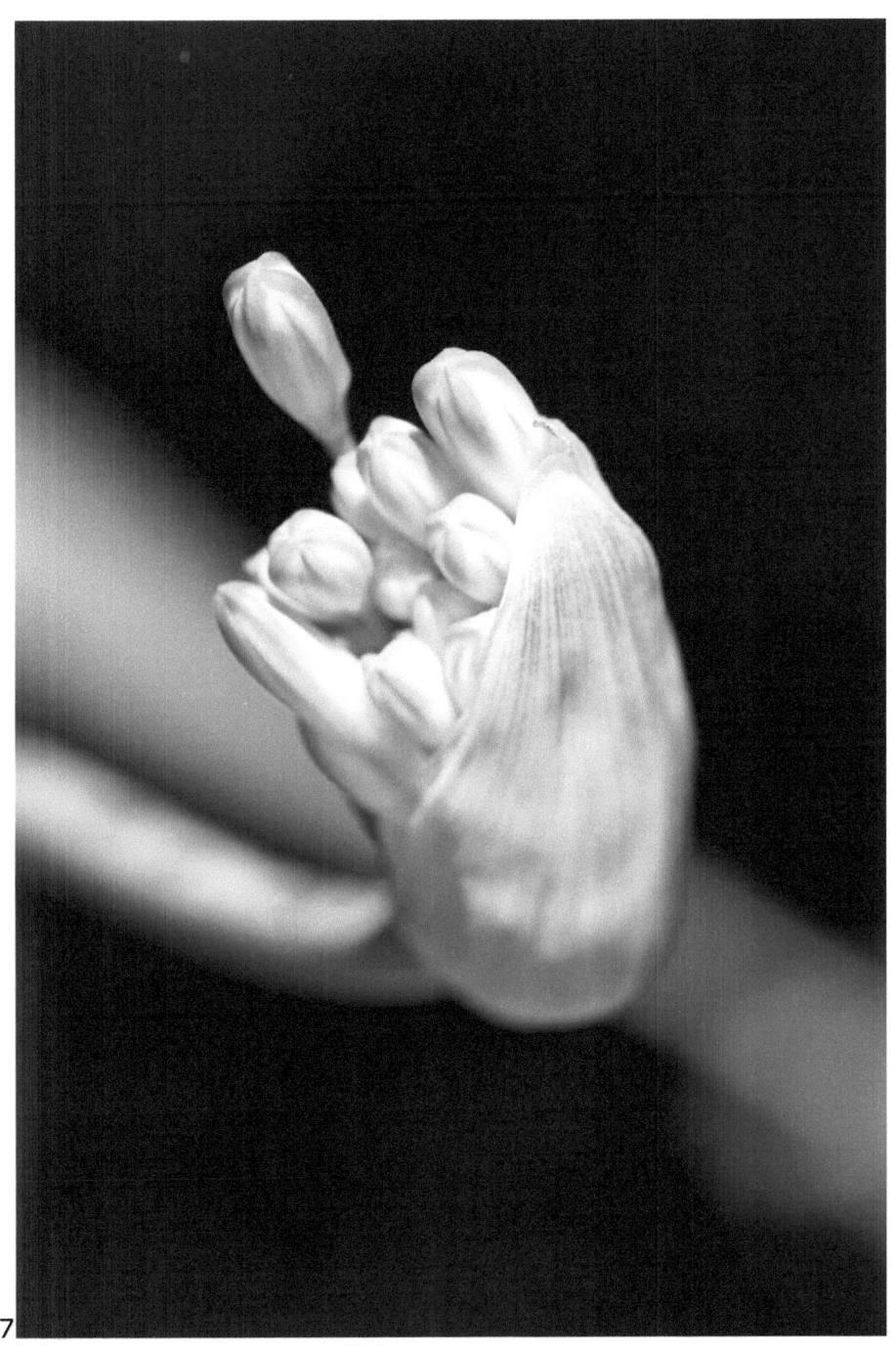

8407

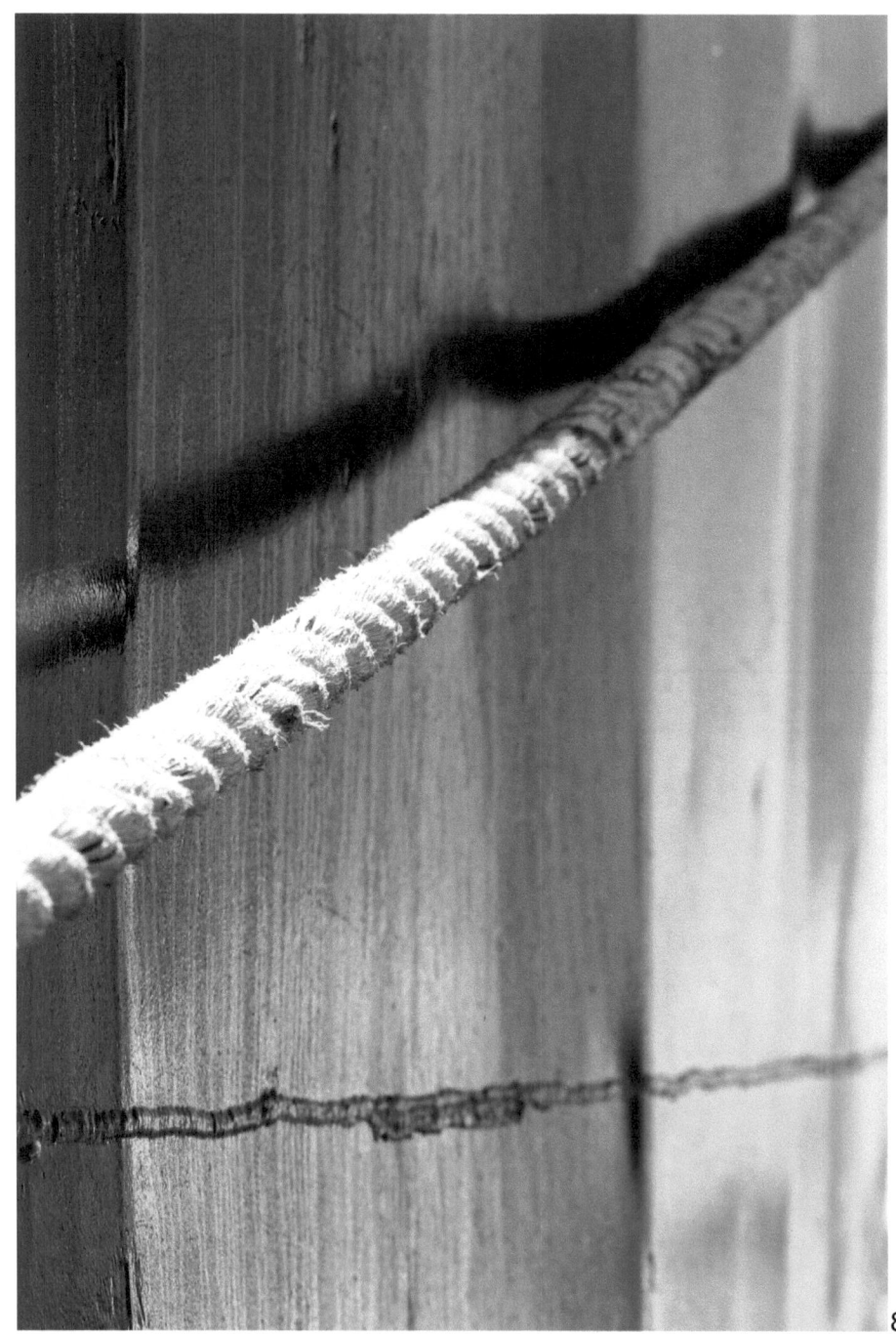

8470

8471

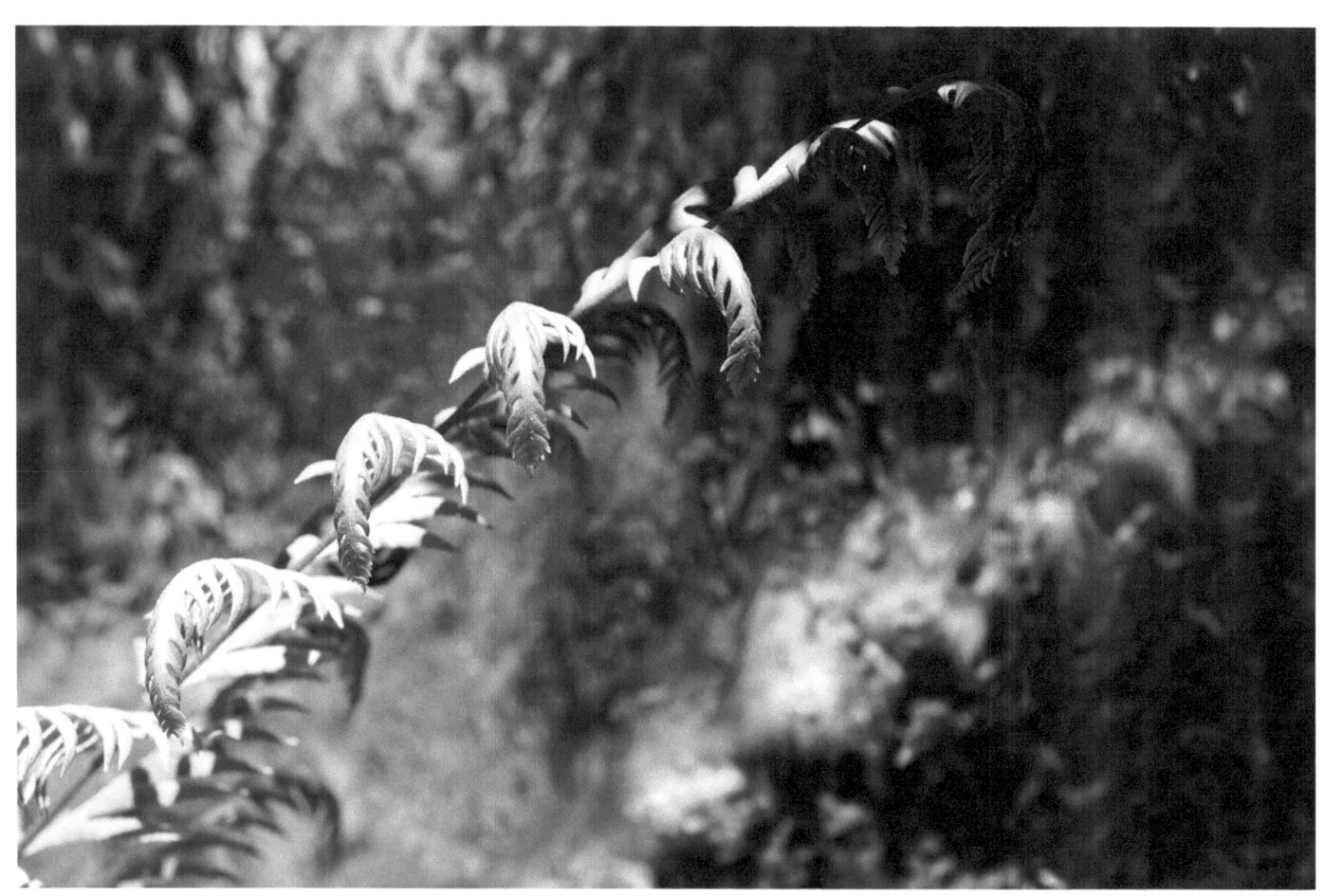

8889

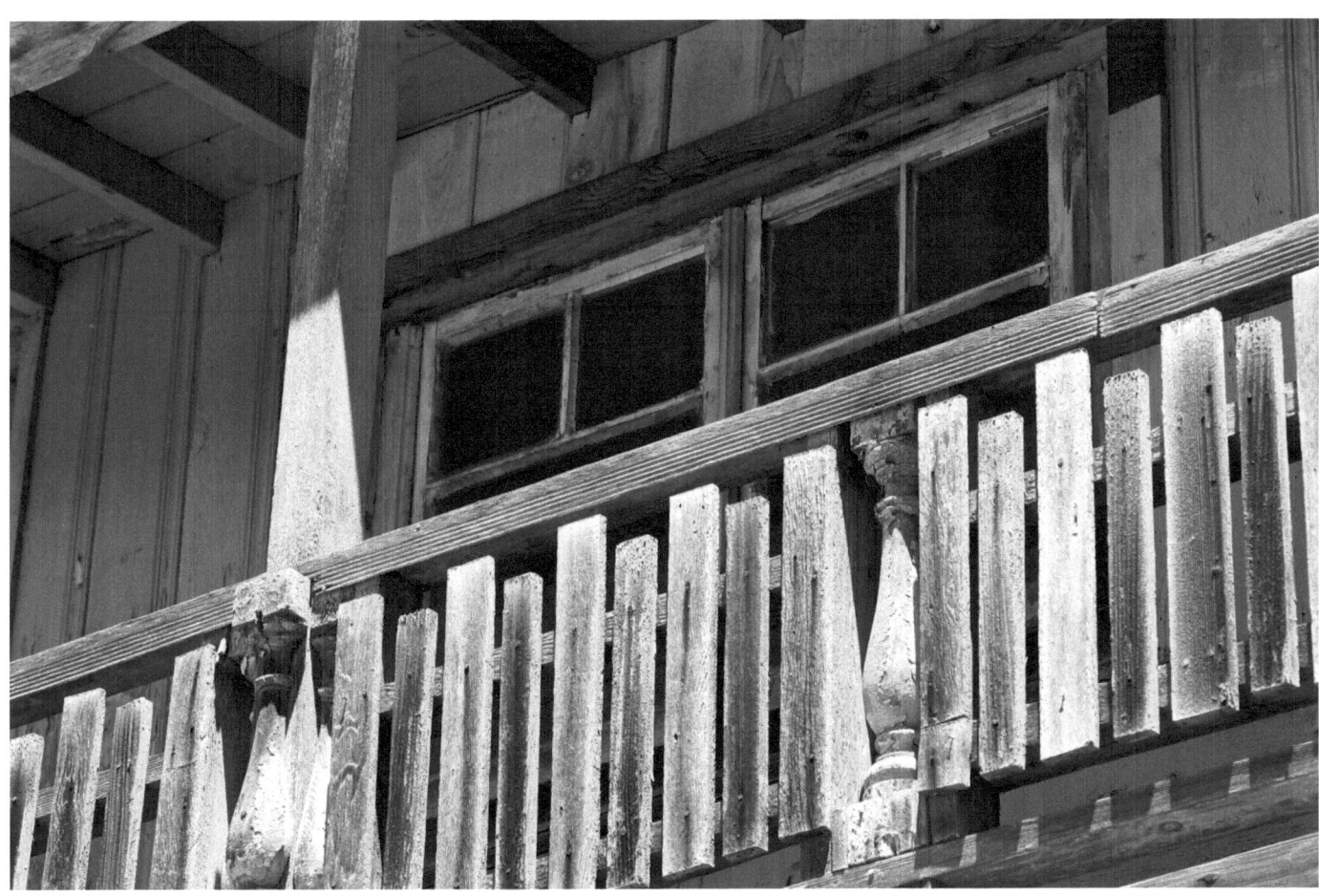

8949

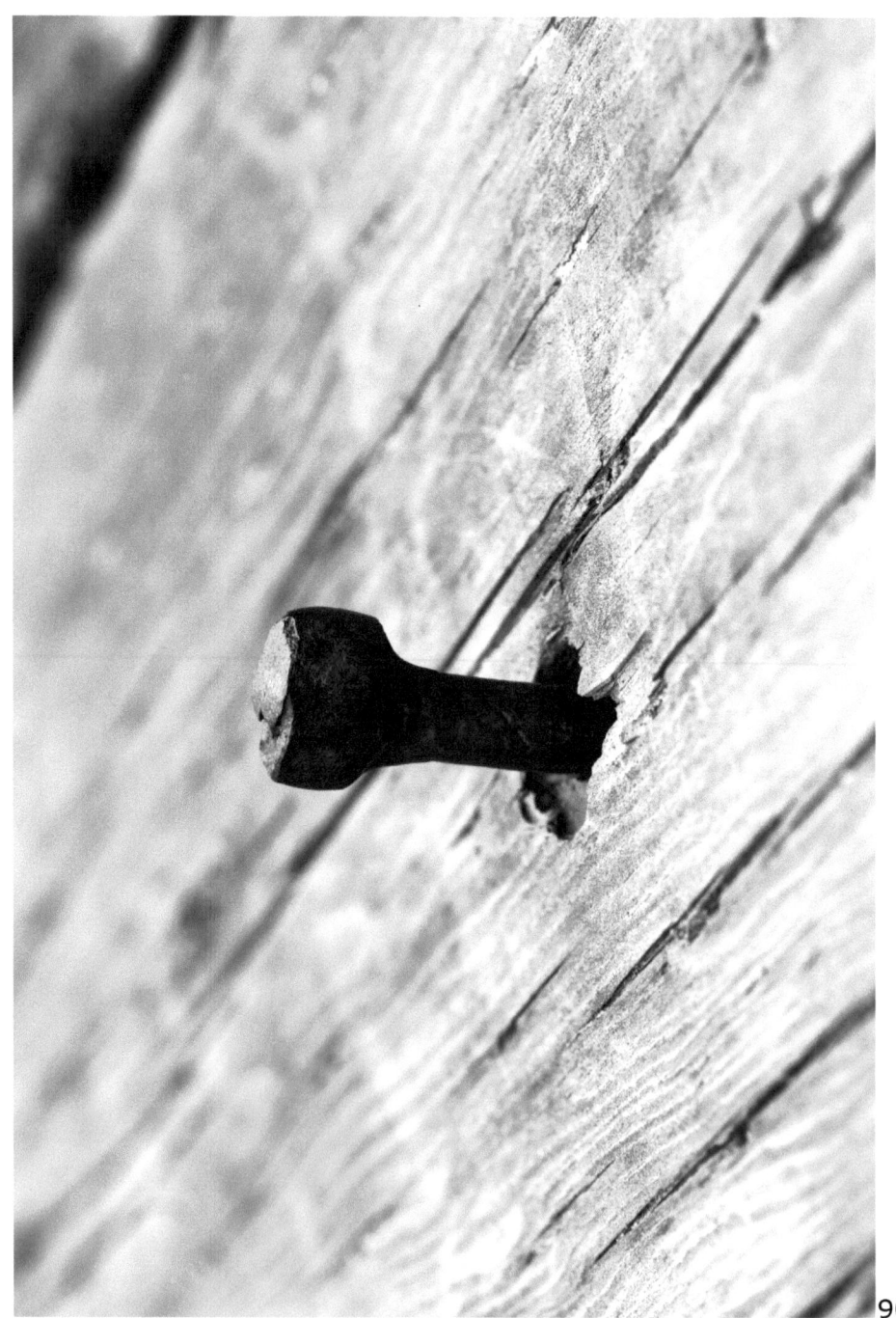

9024

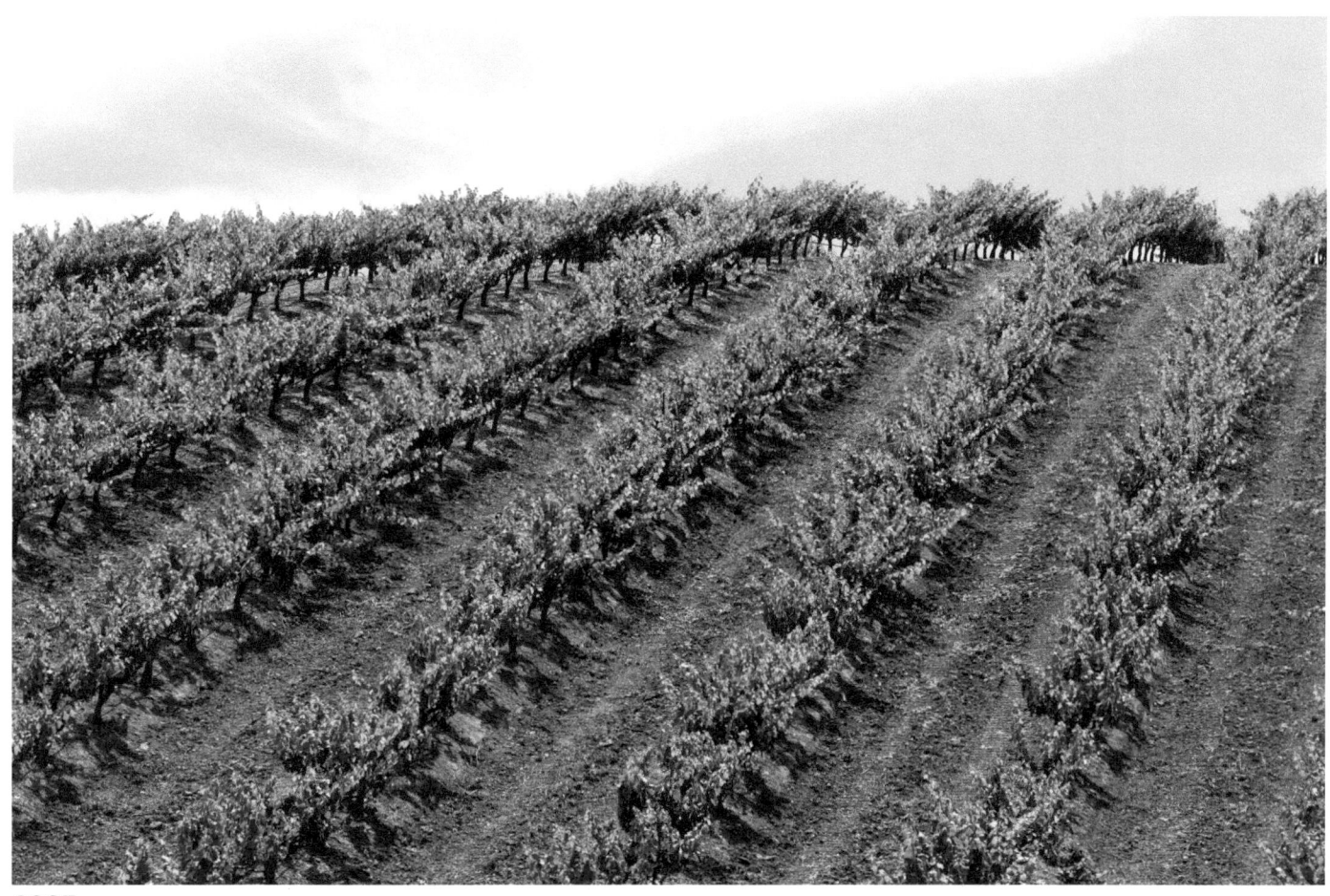

9297

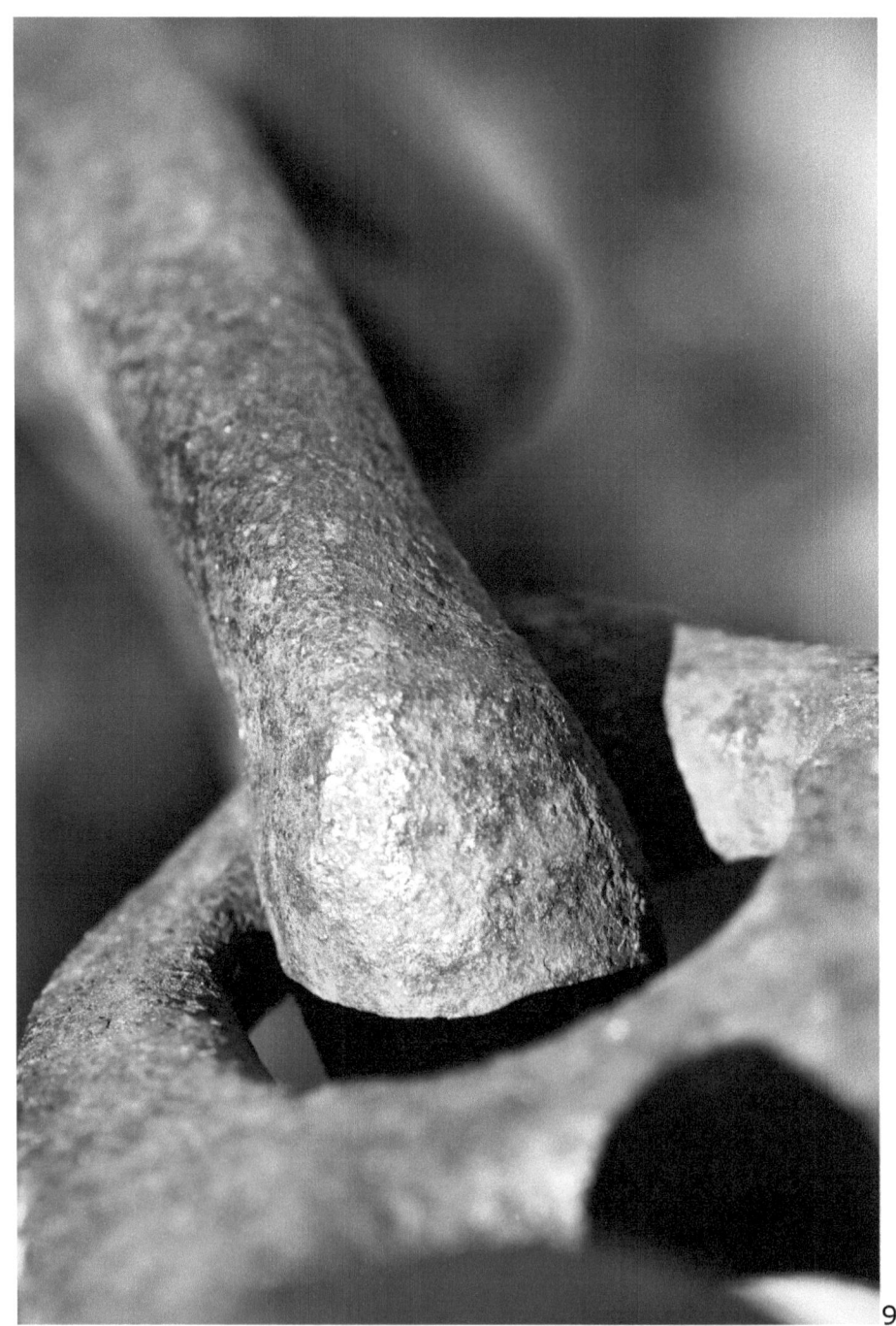

9353

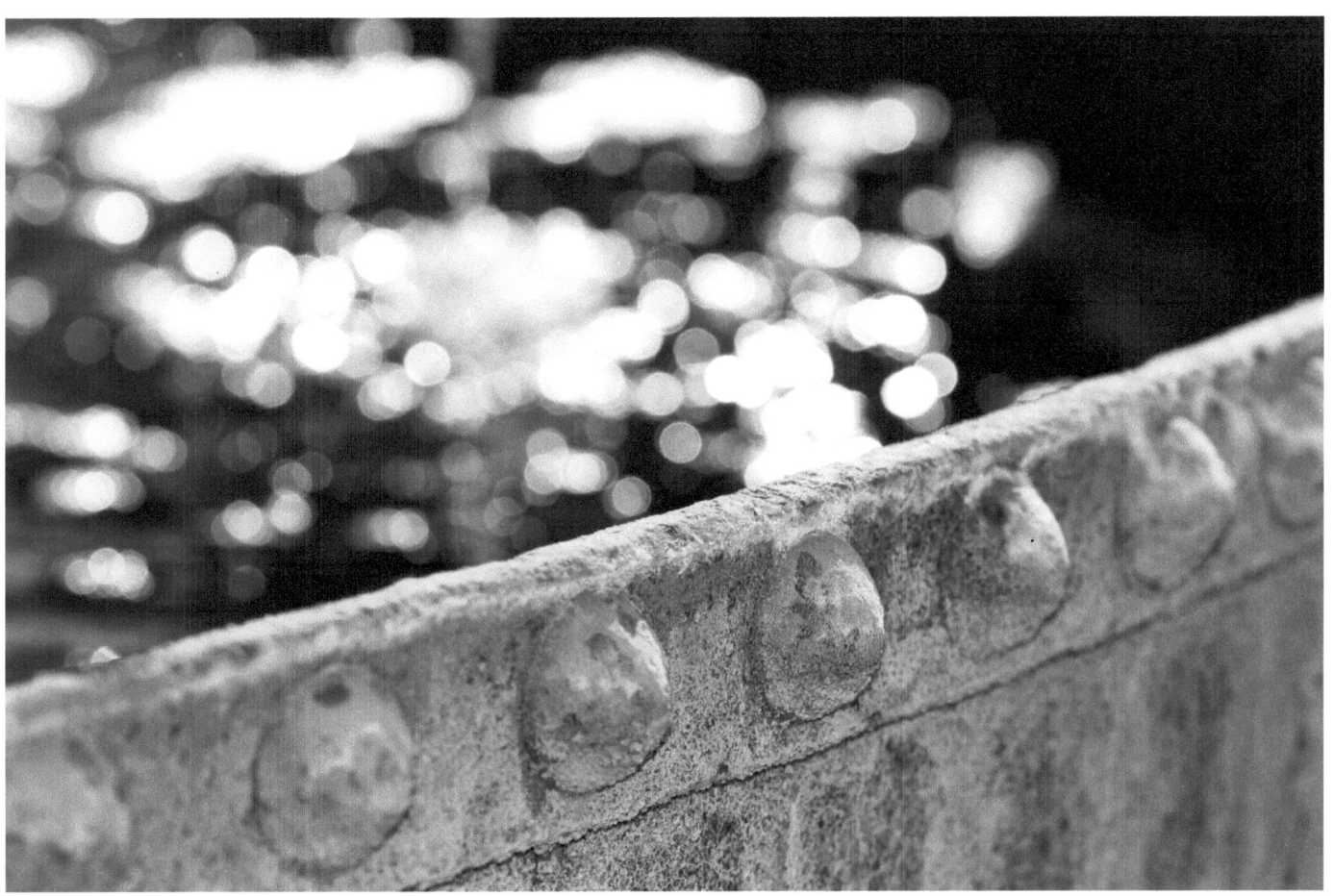

9430

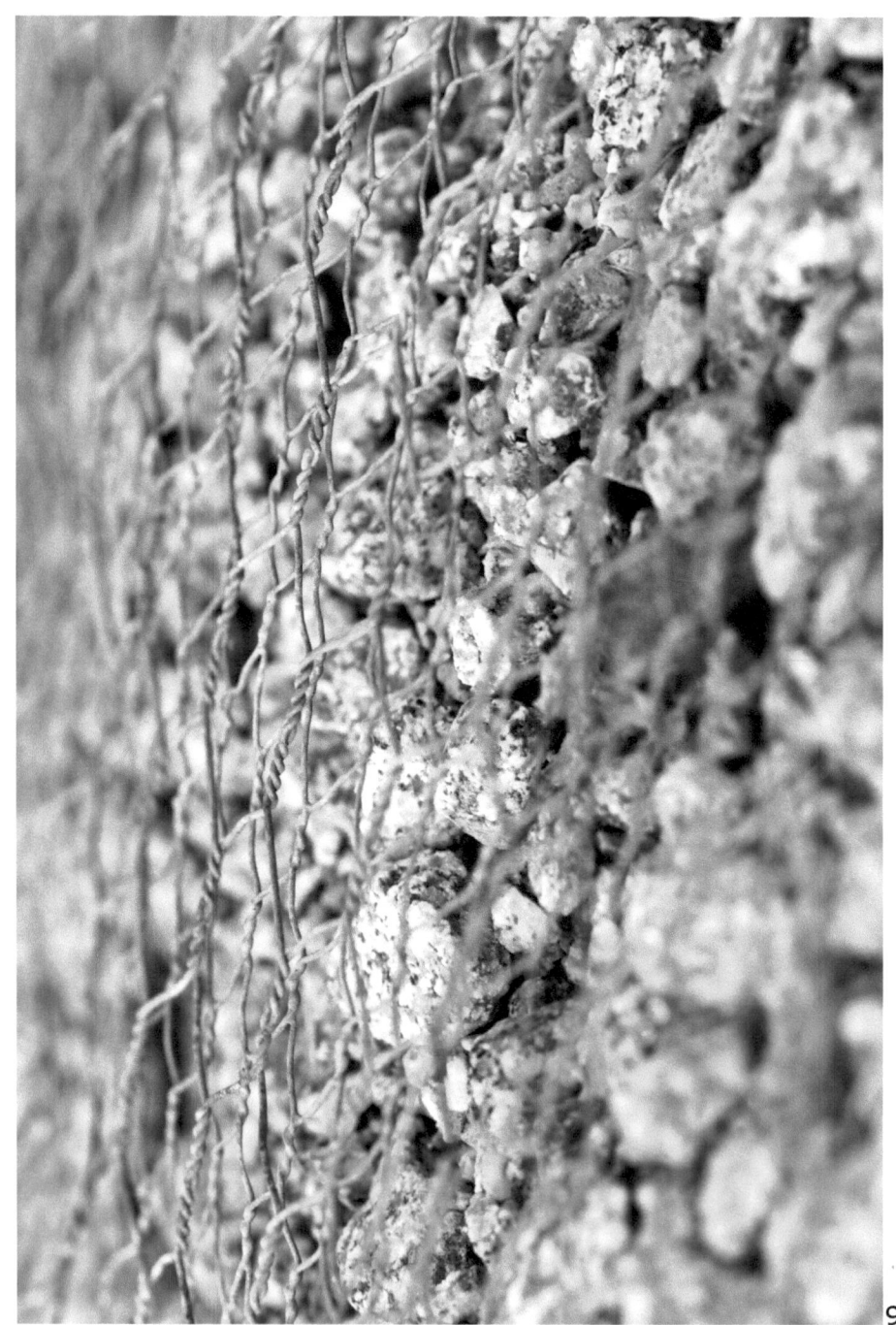

9970

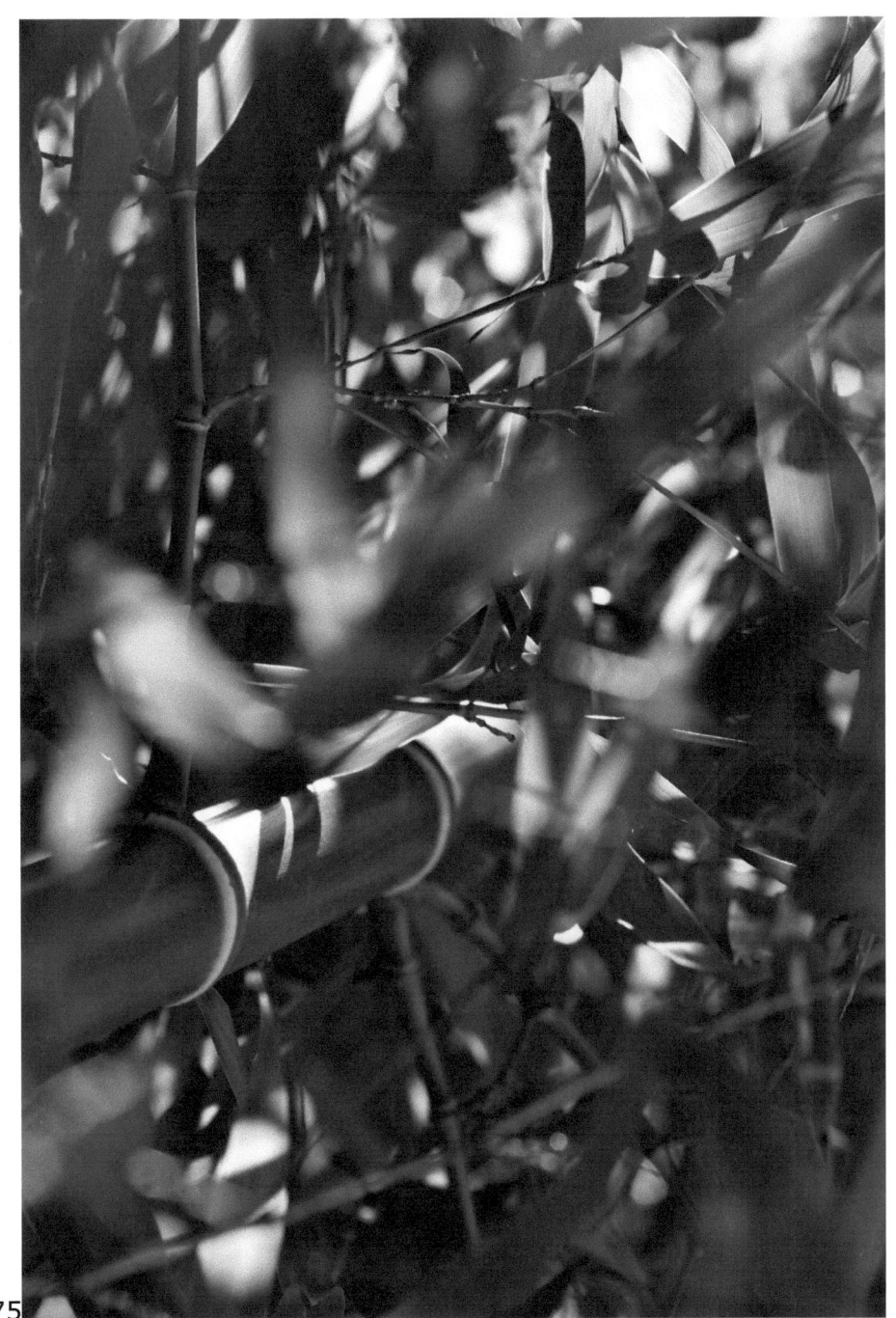

9975

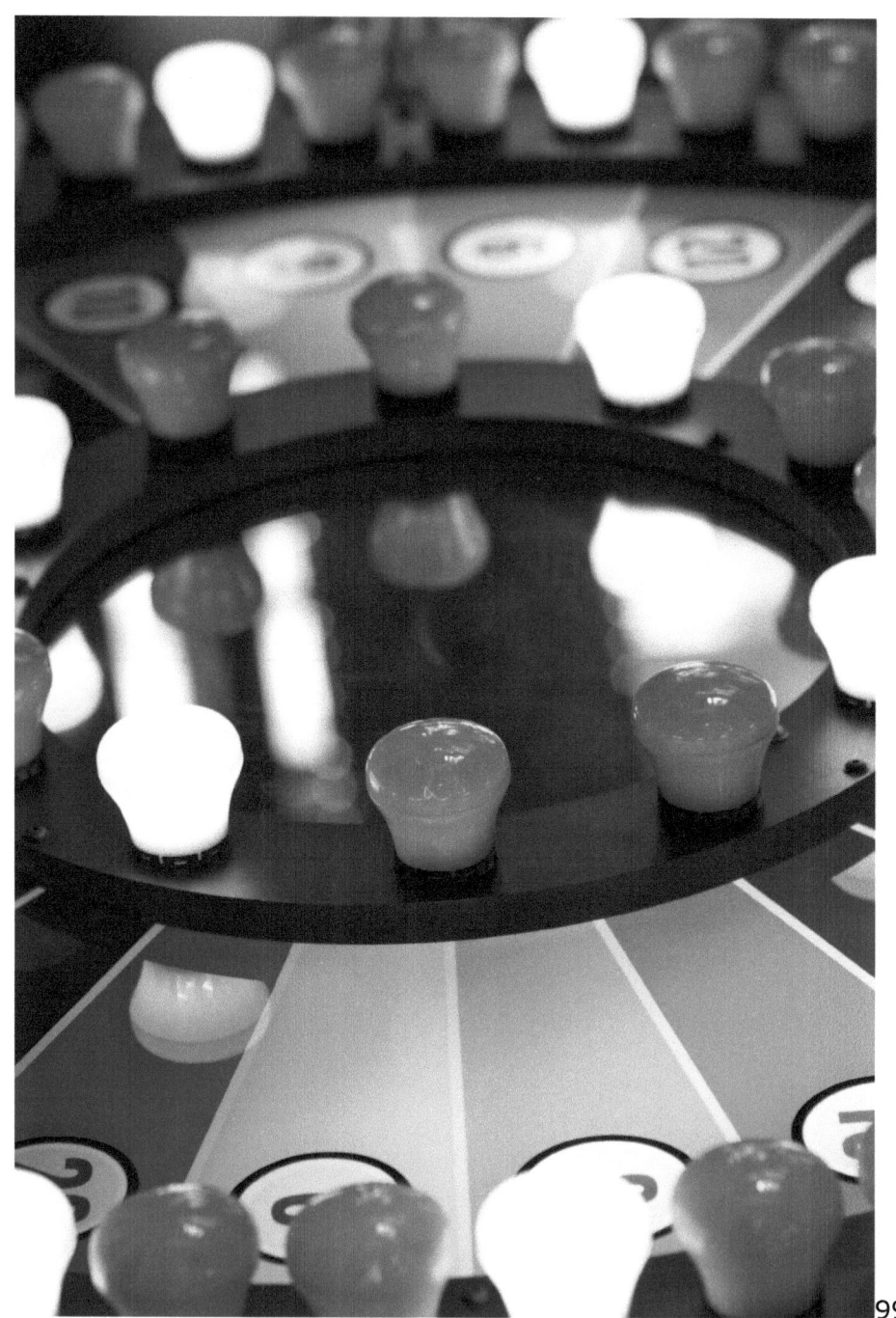

9980

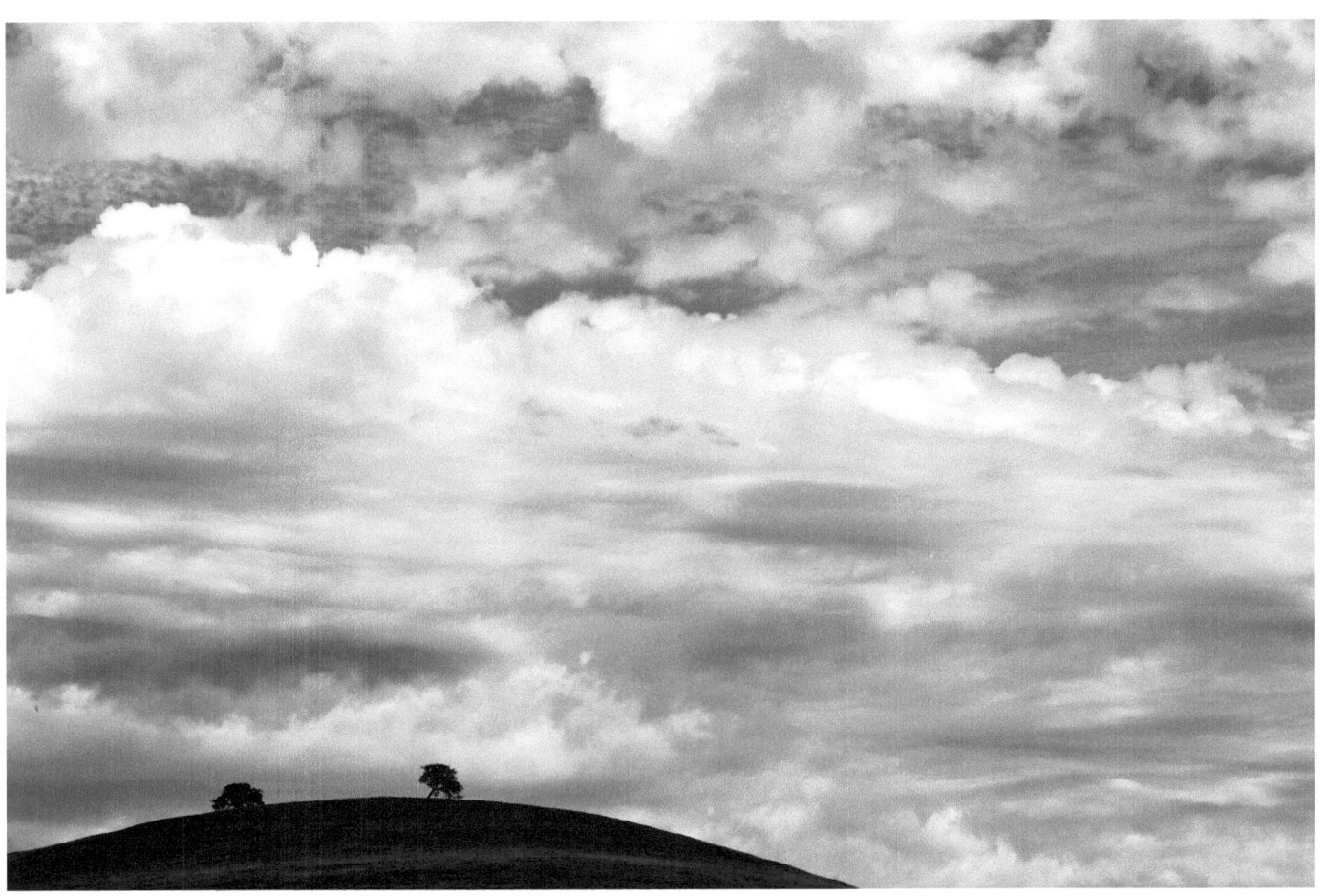

9992

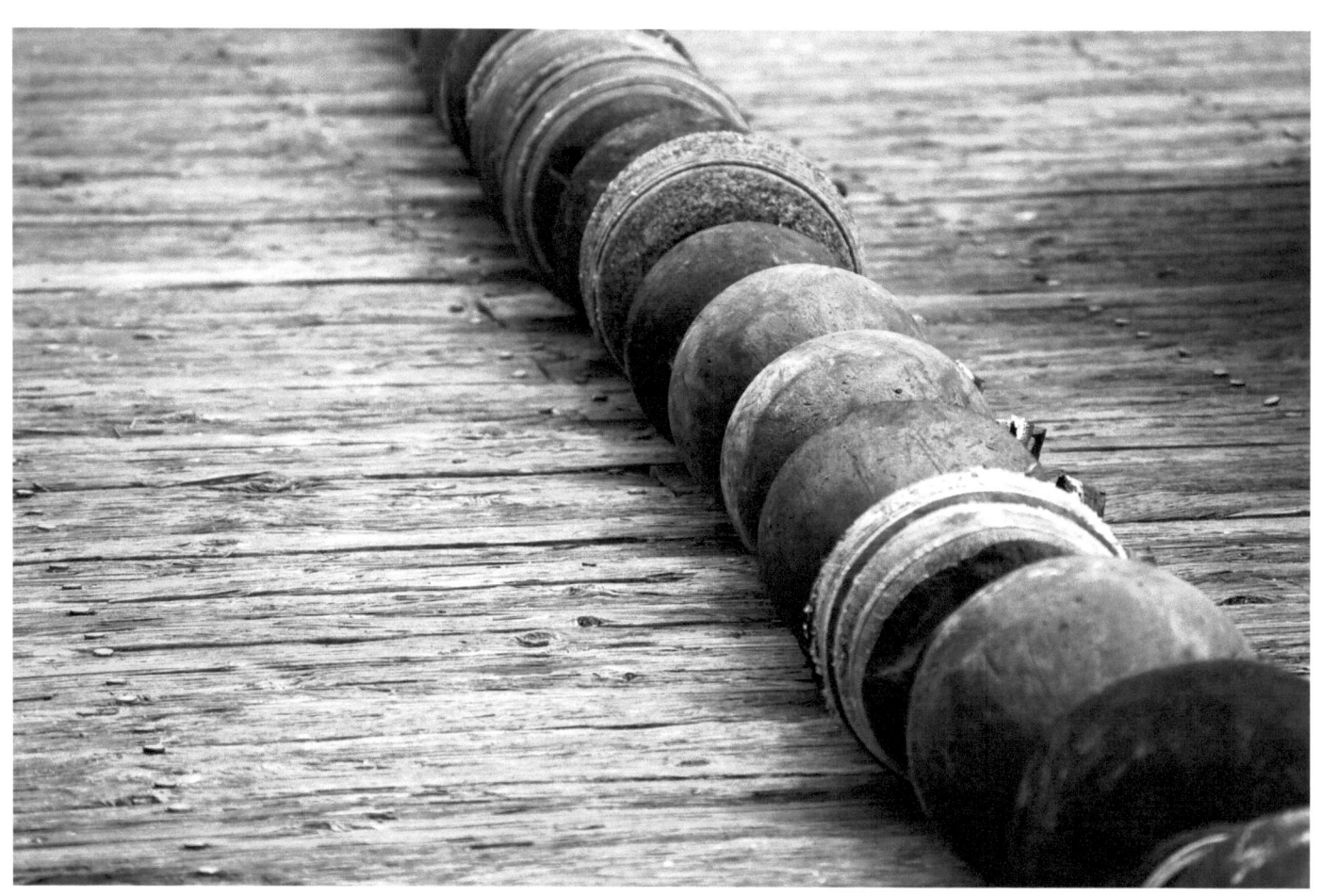

9998

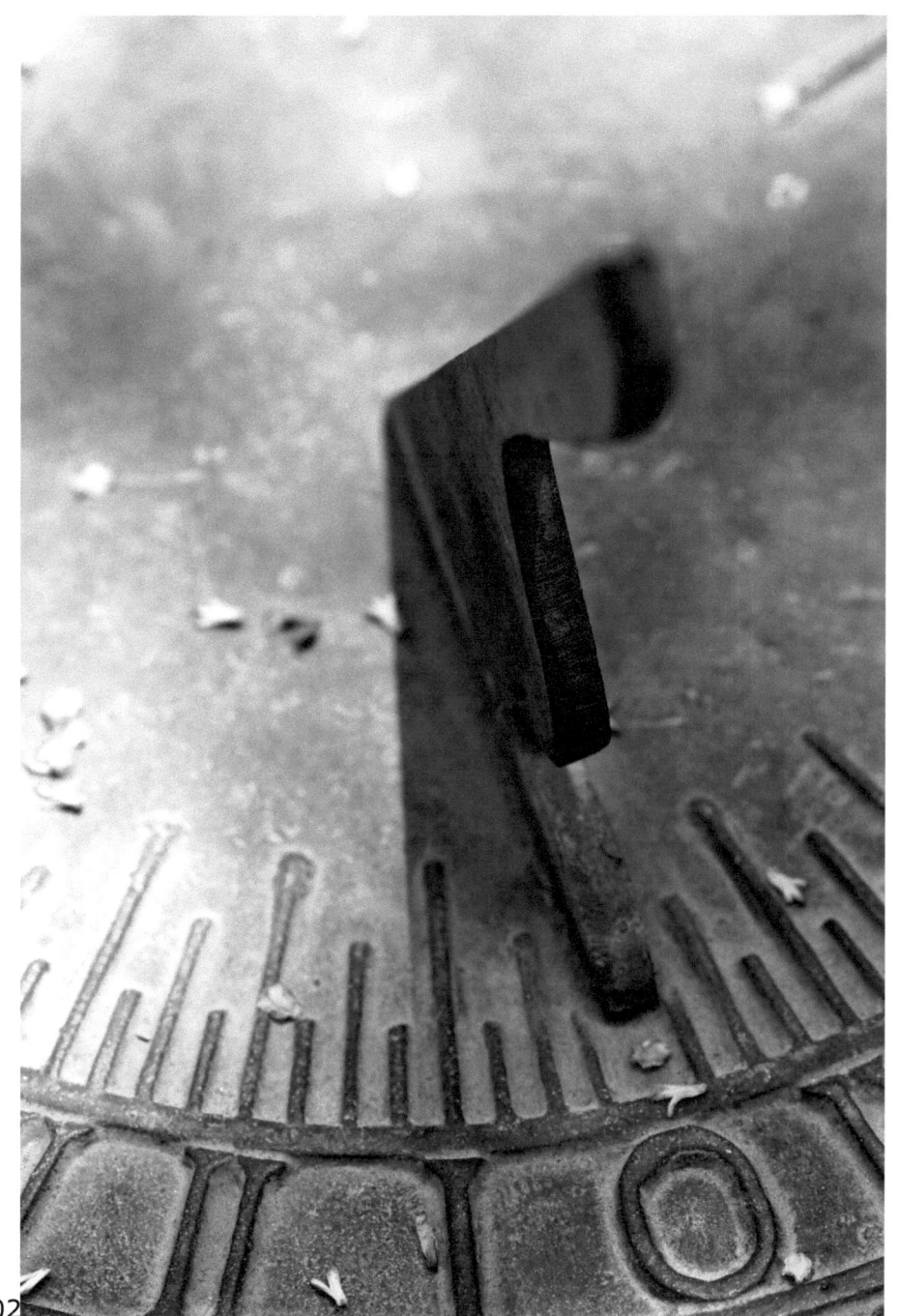

10002

www.ingramcontent.com/pod-product-compliance
Lightning Source LLC
Chambersburg PA
CBHW050742180526
45159CB00003B/1317